uncommon
be extraordinary

.gh school group study

jim burns

general editor

resisting
temptation

Published by Gospel Light
Ventura, California, U.S.A.
www.gospellight.com
Printed in the U.S.A.

Library of Congress Cataloging-in-Publication Data
Uncommon high school group study & leader's guide :
resisting temptation / Jim Burns, general editor.
p. cm.
Originally published: The Word on sex, drugs, rock 'n' Roll.
Ventura, Calif. : Gospel Light, 1994.
Includes bibliographical references and index.
ISBN 978-0-8307-4789-4 (trade paper : alk. paper)
1. Temptation—Study and teaching. 2. Sin—Christianity—Study and teaching.
3. Church work with teenagers. I. Burns, Jim, 1953- II. Title.

BT725.W67 2009
241'.3—dc22
2009034930

Rights for publishing this book outside the U.S.A. or in non-English languages are
administered by Gospel Light Worldwide, an international not-for-profit ministry.
For additional information, please visit www.glww.org, email info@glww.org, or write
to Gospel Light Worldwide, 1957 Eastman Avenue, Ventura, CA 93003, U.S.A.

praise for the
uncommon high school group studies

Jim Burns's work reflects his integrity, intelligence, and his heart for kids. The *Uncommon* high school group studies will change some lives and save many others.

stephen arterburn
Bestselling Author, *Every Man's Battle*

Jim Burns has found the right balance between learning God's Word and applying it to life. The topics are relevant, up to date and on target. Jim gets kids to think. This is a terrific series, and I highly recommend it.

les j. christie
Chair of Youth Ministry, William Jessup University, Rocklin, California

There are very few people in the world who know how to communicate life-changing truth effectively to teens. Jim Burns is one of the best. These studies are biblically sound, hands-on practical and just plain fun. This one gets a five-star endorsement.

ken davis
Author and Speaker (www.kendavis.com)

I don't know anyone who knows and understands the needs of the youth worker like Jim Burns. The *Uncommon* high school group studies are solid, easy to use and get students out of their seats and into the Word.

doug fields
Senior Director of HomeWord Center for Youth and Family @ Azusa Pacific University
Simply Youth Ministry (www.simplyyouthministry.com)

The practicing youth worker always needs more ammunition. The *Uncommon* high school group studies will get that blank stare off the faces of the kids at your youth meeting!

jay kesler
President Emeritus, Taylor University, Upland, Indiana

In the *Uncommon* high school group studies, Jim Burns pulls together the key ingredients for an effective series. He captures the combination of teen involvement and a solid biblical perspective with topics that are relevant and straightforward. This will be a valuable tool in the local church.

dennis "tiger" mcluen
Executive Director, Youth Leadership (www.youthleadership.com)

Young people need the information necessary to make wise decisions related to everyday problems. The *Uncommon* high school group studies will help many young people integrate their faith into everyday life, which, after all, is our goal as youth workers.

miles mcpherson
Senior Pastor, The Rock Church, San Diego, California

This is a resource that is user-friendly, learner-centered and intentionally biblical. I love having a resource like this that I can recommend to youth ministry volunteers and professionals.

duffy robbins
Professor of Youth Ministry, Eastern University, St. Davids, Pennsylvania

The *Uncommon* high school group studies provide the motivation and information for leaders and the types of experience and content that will capture high school people. I recommend it highly.

denny rydberg
President, Young Life (www.younglife.org)

Jim Burns has done it again! This is a practical, timely and reality-based resource for equipping teens to live life in the fast-paced, pressure-packed adolescent world of today.

rich van pelt
President, Compassion International, Denver, Colorado

Jim Burns has his finger on the pulse of youth today. He understands their mindsets and has prepared these studies in a way that will capture their attention and lead them to greater maturity in Christ.

rick warren
Senior Pastor, Saddleback Church, Lake Forest, California
Author of *The Purpose Driven Life*

dedication

To Tom Purcell.
Thank you for your friendship
and partnership in ministry.

There is a friend who sticks closer than a brother.
PROVERBS 18:24

As iron sharpens iron, so one man sharpens another.
PROVERBS 27:17

contents

unit I: resisting sexual temptation

unit II: resisting the temptation of drugs and alcohol

unit III: resisting temptation from the media

how to use
the *uncommon*
group bible studies

Each *Uncommon* Group Bible Study contains 12 sessions, which are divided into 3 stand-alone units of 4 sessions each. You may choose to teach all 12 sessions consecutively, to use just one unit, or to present individual sessions. You know your group, so do what works best for you and your students.

This is your leader's guidebook for teaching your group. Electronic files (in PDF format) of each session's student handouts are available for download at **www.gospellight.com/uncommon/ resisting_temptation.zip**. The handouts include the "message," "dig," "apply," "reflect" and "meditation" sections of each study and have been formatted for easy printing. You may print as many copies as you need for your group.

Each session opens with a devotional meditation written for you, the youth leader. As hectic and trying as youth work is much of the time, it's important never to neglect your interior life. Use the devotions to refocus your heart and prepare yourself to share with kids the message that has already taken root in you. Each of the 12 sessions are divided into the following sections:

starter
Young people will stay in your youth group if they feel comfortable and make friends in the group. This section is designed for you and the students to get to know each other better.

message

The message section will introduce the Scripture reading for the session and get students thinking about how the passage applies to their lives.

dig

Many young people are biblically illiterate. In this section, students will dig into the Word of God and will begin to interact on a personal level with the concepts.

apply

Young people need the opportunity to think through the issues at hand. This section will get students talking about the passage of Scripture and interacting on important issues.

reflect

The conclusion to the study will allow students to reflect on some of the issues presented in the study on a more personal level.

meditation

A closing Scripture for the students to read and reflect on.

unit I

resisting sexual temptation

A study once came across my desk that showed that the average 16-year-old male has a sexual thought every 20 seconds. When I told this statistic to a crowd of high school students, I of course got the usual laughs. However, after the presentation, a young man came up to me and said, "Jim, do you know that quote you said about every 20 seconds a 16-year-old male has a sexual thought?" I looked at him, smiled and said, "Yes." He then asked, "So what am I supposed to think about the other 19 seconds? It's always on my mind!"

Let's face it: Whether we like it or not, people of all ages today are being bombarded with sex and sexual innuendoes in one form or another. Advertisers regularly use sexually explicit material to sell everything from blue jeans to cologne. Young people are particularly susceptible to such come-ons, and this often results in them making poor decisions—and not just in the retail arena. In fact, authorities tell us that teens are making sexual decisions based on these three reasons:

1. *Peer pressure (or the pressure to conform).* You are in the minority if you haven't had sex by age 18.

2. *Emotional involvement that exceeds their maturity level.* Show me a young person with a low self-image who is totally "in love" and I will show you a young person who will be easily seduced sexually.

3. *Lack of value-centered education.* Studies tell us that the more students receive moral and value-centered sex education, the less promiscuous they will be.

Today's Christian young people will have to go against the grain of popular culture to choose a Christ-centered lifestyle of sexuality. It won't be easy for them, and it won't be easy for you to teach the minority view of sexuality in our culture. But keep in mind that when God created male and female, He created all the aspects of personhood—including sexuality—and said, "It is very good" (see Genesis 1–2). And though the Bible is definitely not a sex manual, it does share some very important principles about sex and the need to resist sexual temptations.

This unit is based on the fact that God created sex and that, because He loves us, He wants the best for us. That is why He gives us certain guidelines: He wants us to be all that He created us to be. In this section, you have the opportunity to present biblical sexuality to your students from a positive viewpoint while helping them to "learn to discern" the negative consequences of their actions if they follow the world's standards rather than God's standards.

As you teach this study, you will help young people make important positive decisions about sex before they get into a tempting situation. You will help them work through the incredible amount of mixed messages they are receiving from school, the media, church, home and friends. You will remind them that God created sex and that it's to be approached with Christ-centered principles and values. You will enable young people to make some very important decisions.

As you look at each of the four sessions in this first unit, you will see that we are trying to move teens from accepting the standards of the world to developing a lifestyle of biblical standards and morals when it comes to sexuality and relationships. In each session, you'll have the opportunity to provide information and discuss this topic on a level that young people seldom receive. As you deal with these issues, remember this verse: "It is God's will that you should be sanctified: that you should avoid sexual immorality" (1 Thessalonians 4:3). If you can get even one student to follow this advice, your efforts will have been successful!

One last thought: Thank you for having the courage to bring up this important issue from a Christian point of view with your young people. As you know, young people often have a difficult time distinguishing between their spirituality and their sexuality, and in the next few weeks you will be helping them in both areas of their lives.

is God the great killjoy?

Then God said, "Let us make man in our image, in our likeness,
and let them rule over the fish of the sea and the birds of the air, over the
livestock, over all the earth, and over all the creatures that move along
the ground." God saw all that he had made, and it was very good.
And there was evening, and there was morning—the sixth day.

Genesis 1:26,31

Pretend for a moment that ice cream is your favorite thing in life. You'd almost rather eat ice cream than do anything else. You have become, so to speak, sensitized to ice-cream-related issues. As you watch TV, an incredible array of ice cream sundaes are shown at their richest and most tantalizing. As you drive down the street, you pass shop after shop where you can indulge your passion for ice cream. Billboards showing ice cream melting sweet richness grab your attention. It almost seems as if the whole world is somehow ice cream related!

If you were indeed the person described in the paragraph above, you'd probably eventually come to the conclusion that you were controlled by a passion for ice cream. And the thing you are controlled by, you are also a slave to, according to the apostle Peter (see 2 Peter 2:19).

Now think for a minute about what life was actually like for you as a teenager. A physically healthy teenager is sex-sensitized. Pause for a moment to remember just how deeply influenced you were by all those hormones that God allowed to pump through your veins!

So remember: Before you will sit a group of sensitized young people who need to know more than what *not* to do. They need to understand what God is up to. After all, how could God make them so ready to have sex and yet tell them not to have it? It seems a cruel joke at first. But let's go back to ice cream. It's not ice cream itself that's a problem. Thousands of people never eat ice cream at all. Ice cream can damage you, addict you, even kill you if it's consumed improperly. But in its proper place and proportion, say after a nourishing meal, it's good stuff. In fact, it's great!

Help your students understand that who they are on the *inside* is so important to God that He doesn't want them to misuse anything He's given them. Help them see that sex is good stuff. In fact, it's great! But only in its proper place can it work without damaging and destroying that inner person God loves so much. It's sort of the ice cream that rounds out the meal of a good marriage!

God's plan for our pleasure has never changed. We can be sure that He intended us to experience full satisfaction in the marriage relationship.

ED WHEAT, *INTENDED FOR PLEASURE*

is God the great killjoy?

starter

GOD AND THE BIRDS AND THE BEES: Individually have students answer each of the following questions. They can choose all the answers that apply.

1. My views about sex have been shaped the most by . . .

☐ friends
☐ siblings
☐ parents
☐ pastor/
   youth pastor
☐ church
☐ music

☐ health class/
   sex education
☐ TV/movies
☐ extended family
☐ celebrities
☐ own experiences
☐ magazines

☐ boyfriend or
   girlfriend
☐ _____
☐ _____
☐ _____
☐ _____
☐ _____

Note: You can download this group study guide in 8¹/₂" x 11" format at
www.gospellight.com/uncommon/resisting_temptation.zip.

2. I think that God views sex as . . .

☐ dirty   ☐ a way to produce   ☐ a gift
☐ beautiful   offspring   ☐ not to be enjoyed
☐ a topic that   ☐ meant for   ☐ _____
   shouldn't be   married couples   ☐ _____
   talked about   ☐ shameful   ☐ _____

3. Do you agree or disagree with the following statements?

(A)   (D)
☐   ☐   It's hard for me to think about God in relation to
            my sexuality.
☐   ☐   Abstinence before marriage is just a suggestion in
            the Bible.
☐   ☐   God created sex just as a way for people to produce
            children.
☐   ☐   Within His guidelines, God wants people to en-
            joy sex.
☐   ☐   God plays a big role in determining the direction
            and activities of my sexuality.
☐   ☐   These days, it's not possible to remain a virgin un-
            til you are married.
☐   ☐   I believe that my sexuality is one way that I can
            demonstrate my faith.

message

Some people have the perception that God doesn't want us to
have sex, talk about sex or even think about it. But God created
sex. He designed it and built it to work in a specific way. Know-

ing and understanding what God says about sex will give us strength as we strive for sexual purity and will lead us to wholeness in our sexuality.

Read the following passages in Genesis 1:26-31 and 2:18-25. As you read, keep the following questions in mind: (1) What do these verses reveal about how God viewed His creation of humankind? (2) What was the purpose for man and woman being brought together as "one flesh" (verse 24)?

Then God said, "Let us make man in our image, in our likeness, and let them rule over the fish of the sea and the birds of the air, over the livestock, over all the earth, and over all the creatures that move along the ground."

So God created man in his own image, in the image of God he created him; male and female he created them.

God blessed them and said to them, "Be fruitful and increase in number; fill the earth and subdue it. Rule over the fish of the sea and the birds of the air and over every living creature that moves on the ground."

Then God said, "I give you every seed-bearing plant on the face of the whole earth and every tree that has fruit with seed in it. They will be yours for food. And to all the beasts of the earth and all the birds of the air and all the creatures that move on the ground—everything that has the breath of life in it—I give every green plant for food." And it was so.

God saw all that he had made, and it was very good. And there was evening, and there was morning—the sixth day. . . .

The Lord God said, "It is not good for the man to be alone. I will make a helper suitable for him."

Now the Lord God had formed out of the ground all the beasts of the field and all the birds of the air. He brought them to the man to see what he would name them; and whatever the man called each living creature, that was its name. So the man gave names to all the livestock, the birds of the air and all the beasts of the field.

But for Adam no suitable helper was found. So the Lord God caused the man to fall into a deep sleep; and while he was sleeping, he took one of the man's ribs and closed up the place with flesh. Then the Lord God made a woman from the rib he had taken out of the man, and he brought her to the man.

The man said, "This is now bone of my bones and flesh of my flesh; she shall be called 'woman,' for she was taken out of man."

For this reason a man will leave his father and mother and be united to his wife, and they will become one flesh.

The man and his wife were both naked, and they felt no shame.

dig

1. Genesis 1:26 says, "Let us make man in our image, in our likeness." What does it mean that we are made in the likeness of God? What about us is the same? (Notice that the verse uses "us" and "our." This passage is one of the illustrations of the triune nature of God—Father, Son and Holy Spirit.)

2. How do you think being made in God's image relates to our sexuality?

_____

_____

_____

_____

_____

_____

3. According to the passage, why did God create woman?

_____

_____

_____

_____

_____

_____

4. Before the Fall, God reveals His ideal situation for a man and his wife. Read Genesis 2:24-25. What is God's plan for the sexual relationship between a man and his wife?

_____

_____

_____

_____

_____

5. Beyond just having sexual intercourse, what does "become one flesh" mean (see verse 24)?

    ....

    ....

    ....

    ....

    ....

6. Some people are unclear about what God specifically approves or disapproves of in regard to our sexuality. Read and summarize in your own words what God says about each of the following situations, and then think about the negative consequences for each of the actions.

    Adultery: voluntary sexual intercourse between a married person and a partner who is not the husband or wife.

    Exodus 20:14

    ....

    ....

    ....

    ....

    Proverbs 6:32-33

    ....

    ....

    ....

    ....

Matthew 5:28

_____
_____
_____
_____
_____

Consequences (physical, emotional, spiritual)

_____
_____
_____
_____
_____

Sexual immorality or fornication: sexual intercourse between unmarried partners.

Romans 13:12-14

_____
_____
_____
_____

1 Corinthians 6:18-20

_____
_____
_____
_____

1 Thessalonians 4:3-6

_____

_____

_____

_____

_____

Consequences (physical, emotional, spiritual)

_____

_____

_____

_____

_____

Separating one flesh: Tearing apart two who have become one. Sexual intercourse is the most graphic illustration of two people literally joined (bodily, spiritually and emotionally) as one.

Matthew 19:4-6

_____

_____

_____

_____

_____

_____

1 Corinthians 6:15-16

_____

_____

_____

_____

_____

_____

Consequences (physical, emotional, spiritual)

_____

_____

_____

_____

_____

_____

apply

1. What is a godly view of sex?

_____

_____

_____

_____

_____

_____

_____

_____

2. Your friend Terri is a student leader in the church youth group. As a student leader, she has made a commitment to not have sexual intercourse until marriage. However, she has fallen in love with Ron, and they have been going further and further in their physical relationship. Terri does love Ron and believes one day they will get married, but she wants to live her life by Christian principles, so she comes to you for help and advice. Write a letter of advice to Terri.

Dear Terri,

_____

_____

_____

_____

_____

_____

_____

3. Circle the following actions in the list below that are useful techniques for finding out God's direction and guidance for your sexuality.

    *   talking about it with my friends
    *   asking God through prayer
    *   asking my parents
    *   talking with my youth pastor
    *   seeing how the media portrays sexuality
    *   seeing what feels "right" in the moment
    *   following the motto, "If it's not intercourse, then it's probably okay"
    *   reading Scripture

reflect

1. If God created sex and He sees it as very good, why would
    He ask us to wait until marriage to have sexual intercourse?

    _____

    _____

    _____

    _____

    _____

2. What are the benefits of waiting until marriage to have
    sexual intercourse?

    _____

    _____

    _____

    _____

    _____

3. Although sex is a gift from God, some people overempha-
    size sex. Why is overemphasizing sex an ungodly view?

    _____

    _____

    _____

    _____

    _____

    _____

4. Some people view sex as dirty, even within the confines of
    marriage. Why is this an ungodly view?

    _____

    _____

    _____

    _____

    _____

    _____

5. How can a person create and maintain a godly view of sex?

    _____

    _____

    _____

    _____

    _____

    _____

6. What are some of the physical consequences of having
    premarital sex?

    _____

    _____

    _____

    _____

    _____

    _____

7. What are some of the spiritual and emotional consequences
    of premarital sex?

    _____

    _____

    _____

    _____

    _____

    _____

    _____

    _____

meditation

Create in me a pure heart, O God,
and renew a steadfast spirit within me.

PSALM 51:10

session 2

influences

*Do not merely listen to the word, and so
deceive yourselves. Do what it says.*

JAMES 1:22

Through many generations of books, magazines, songs, plays, movies and the Internet, society has sent all of us a subtle yet powerful—and extremely damaging—message about sex and about relationship: Sex can be divorced from relationship and still satisfy. Sex is often portrayed as a one-dimensional act of physical performance, making relationship not only unnecessary but also undesirable. The irony is that an opposite message is often sent at the same time—that this sexual performance somehow will *create* relationship between two people. Is it any wonder that we've all been a bit confused at some point?

The damage and confusion contrast powerfully with the value God places on relationship. He has focused all His love and grace on establishing valuable relationship between Himself and us! He has given us the power as His children to foster and to value healthy relationships among ourselves. Relationship is number one with Him!

Before teaching this particular session, check your own personal relationship index. Consider what other conflicting messages may be sent—by us, adult leaders. Remember that even with young people this age, more is still "caught than taught." As we teach, our body language, tone of voice and the attitudes we display will tell more than what we say! What are your true feelings about these students to whom you relate? What is *your* honest attitude toward sex? Your genuine feelings about male-female relationships? Your true attitude toward the media?

The attitudes we show need to exemplify what we say about the value of relationship and about the value God places on each of us! Ask God to shape your nonverbal teaching as well as your words into the unmixed message of loving relationship that He wants your teens to see—and from which they'll learn.

The media doesn't make it seem like it's really all about love. Nowadays sexuality is the way you look. . . . It's all physical, not what's inside you.
SEVENTEEN-YEAR-OLD GIRL

influences

starter

SURROUNDED: have students divide into three groups. Have each group examine how sexual messages and images surround and influence us.

Group 1: Think of TV commercials that use sex and sexual innuendos in one form or another to sell their products. Make a list of the products being sold and how sex is used to sell them.

Group 2: Look through a magazine (sports, fashion, news, music and so forth) to find blatant and subtle examples of how advertisers use sex to sell their products. Mark the ad pages with Post-it Notes.

Group 3: List as many song titles you can think of that use subtle or blatant references to sex. See how many song titles you can come up with.

Have each group answer the following questions: (1) Why do advertisers/artists use sex to sell their product? (2) What is the impact of this approach on the viewer/listener?

message

The first chapter in Genesis describes how God created earth and sky, light and water, man and beast. The second chapter describes how God gave Adam and Eve responsibilities (take care of the Garden and the animals) and some rules—specifically, He told them not to eat fruit from one tree in the Garden of Eden. According to the Bible, this is the ONE rule He gave to Adam and Eve—and, as you may have heard, they had a little trouble keeping it.

Read the following account from Genesis 3:1-13. As you read, consider the following questions: (1) What were Adam and Eve's intentions? Did they plan on breaking God's rule? (2) How much convincing did it take to get them to disobey?

Now the serpent was more crafty than any of the wild animals the Lord God had made. He said to the woman, "Did God really say, 'You must not eat from any tree in the garden'?"

The woman said to the serpent, "We may eat fruit from the trees in the garden, but God did say, 'You must not eat fruit from the tree that is in the middle of the garden, and you must not touch it, or you will die.'"

"You will not surely die," the serpent said to the woman. "For God knows that when you eat of it your eyes will be opened, and you will be like God, knowing good and evil."

When the woman saw that the fruit of the tree was good for food and pleasing to the eye, and also desirable for gaining wis-

dom, she took some and ate it. She also gave some to her husband, who was with her, and he ate it. Then the eyes of both of them were opened, and they realized they were naked; so they sewed fig leaves together and made coverings for themselves.

Then the man and his wife heard the sound of the Lord God as he was walking in the garden in the cool of the day, and they hid from the Lord God among the trees of the garden. But the Lord God called to the man, "Where are you?"

He answered, "I heard you in the garden, and I was afraid because I was naked; so I hid."

And he said, "Who told you that you were naked? Have you eaten from the tree that I commanded you not to eat from?"

The man said, "The woman you put here with me—she gave me some fruit from the tree, and I ate it."

Then the Lord God said to the woman, "What is this you have done?"

The woman said, "The serpent deceived me, and I ate."

dig

1. What were Adam and Eve influenced by?

_____

_____

_____

_____

_____

_____

_____

_____

2. What was the result of them following that influence?

    _____

    _____

    _____

    _____

    _____

    _____

3. Adam and Eve knew what was right. They weren't con-
    fused about what God had commanded them to do, and
    they planned to obey. Yet they still were led astray. Why
    did Adam and Eve fall prey to the serpent's influence?

    _____

    _____

    _____

    _____

    _____

    _____

4. How could they have avoided the temptation?

    _____

    _____

    _____

    _____

    _____

    _____

5. Influences are not inherently bad. Positive influences can play an important role in our lives. But because of the actions of Adam and Eve, every single person is born with a sinful nature. And this sinful nature can be easily tempted by negative influences. What do these passages reveal about our sinful nature?

Romans 7:18

Romans 8:5

Galatians 5:16-17

Galatians 6:7-8

1 Peter 2:11

....
....
....
....

apply

Everyone is influenced when it comes to the subject of sexuality.
The question is who and what are influencing you.

1. Whether we like it or not, those things that we spend the
    most time listening to, watching and being around will
    undoubtedly impact our views and beliefs. What gets
    most of your time and attention today? Rate from 1 (the
    most influential) to 13 (the least influential) the follow-
    ing things and people in regard to their influence on you.

    Music   ....
    TV   ....
    Parent   ....
    Brother/Sister   ....
    Movies   ....
    Government   ....
    Youth Worker   ....
    Teachers   ....
    Friends   ....
    Books   ....
    Church   ....
    Advertisements   ....
    Bible   ....

2. Look at what you ranked as the top three things and/or people that influence you. What messages about sex and sexuality do these influences promote?

_____
_____
_____
_____
_____
_____
_____
_____

3. Why do these influences hold so much sway over people your age?

_____
_____
_____
_____
_____
_____
_____
_____

4. One of the major influences of today's teens is the media. Though you may not realize it, when we consistently see certain images, attitudes or behaviors portrayed on TV and in films, we begin to view them as acceptable or at

least as not that bad. On the Internet, search for episode descriptions of the following shows from different decades:

1960s: *Leave It to Beaver, Gilligan's Island, The Dick Van Dyke Show*

1970s: *The Partridge Family, Eight Is Enough, The Brady Bunch*

1980s: *Full House, Saved by the Bell, Family Ties*

1990s: *Clueless, Melrose Place, 90210*

2000s: *Gossip Girl, One Tree Hill, The Hills*

Do you notice a shift in the content of the shows? When we continue to see as normal things like premarital sex, couples living together before marriage and promiscuous teens, how we view sexuality in our own life is influenced.

5. Check the box if you've heard or seen of any of the following being portrayed on TV shows or in movies:

☐ adultery

☐ individuals going further physically than they originally wanted to

☐ teenagers having multiple sexual partners

☐ people viewing pornography

☐ provocative or seductive dancing

☐ blatant or implied sexual intercourse

☐ sexual touching

☐ non-married couples living together

☐ one-night stands

☐ heavy kissing

☐ someone cheating on a boyfriend or a girlfriend

6. Read Philippians 4:8. What does the Bible say about all inappropriate behavior?

    _____

    _____

    _____

    _____

    _____

    _____

    _____

7. Why does what we fill our brains with through media, music and friends matter?

    _____

    _____

    _____

    _____

    _____

    _____

    _____

8. Read the following verses aloud and then summarize them in your own words.

    You have heard that it was said, "Do not commit adultery." But I tell you that anyone who looks at a woman lustfully has already committed adultery with her in his heart. If your right eye causes you to sin, gouge it out and throw it away. It is better for you to lose one part of your body than for your whole body to be thrown into hell. And if your right hand causes you to sin, cut it off and throw it away. It is better for you to lose one part of your body than for your whole body to go into hell (Matthew 5:27-30).

But among you there must not be even a hint of sexual immorality, or of any kind of impurity, or of greed, because these are improper for God's holy people. Nor should there be obscenity, foolish talk or coarse joking, which are out of place, but rather thanksgiving. For of this you can be sure: No immoral, impure or greedy person—such a man is an idolater—has any inheritance in the kingdom of Christ and of God (Ephesians 5:3-5).

9. Based on these passages, develop a list of God's standards for the TV, movies and music we consume.

1. _____

2. _____

3. _____

4. _____

5. _____

reflect

1. What is your own view of sexuality?

_____

_____

_____

_____

_____

_____

_____

2. What influences have shaped your understanding of and views on sexuality?

_____

_____

_____

_____

_____

_____

3. Is it okay for actors and actresses to act in the nude or in sexually explicit scenes since they are "only acting"? Why or why not?

    _____

    _____

    _____

    _____

    _____

4. Do you think Christians should view sexually explicit films? Why or why not? Would the age or maturity of the viewer be a factor in this regard?

    _____

    _____

    _____

    _____

    _____

5. Why do you think movies today contain so much sexually explicit material? What is its purpose?

    _____

    _____

    _____

    _____

    _____

    _____

6. Do you believe that the movies present an accurate por-
    trayal of sexuality and male/female relationships?

    _____

    _____

    _____

    _____

    _____

    _____

7. Who or what in our culture is portraying a positive bibli-
    cal view of sexuality?

    _____

    _____

    _____

    _____

    _____

    _____

8. A friend says, "There's no harm in just *watching* that kind
    of stuff. I'm not actually doing it." How would you re-
    spond? Is there harm in "just watching"?

    _____

    _____

    _____

    _____

    _____

9. Do you agree (A) or disagree (D) with the following state-
    ments? Respond and then discuss your answers as a group.

(A)   (D)

☐   ☐   I need to be proactive about developing a healthy
            and godly view of sex.

☐   ☐   Parents make too big a deal about the sex that
            is on TV and in movies.

☐   ☐   As a Christian, my views about sexuality should
            be different from those of the secular world.

☐   ☐   I gather most of what I know and think about
            sex from TV and movies.

☐   ☐   Even though I see sex portrayed in films and TV,
            my personal views and behavior aren't affected.

☐   ☐   One way that my friends can see Christ in my
            life is through my decisions regarding sexuality.

☐   ☐   My views and actions regarding sexuality impact
            my effectiveness as a witness for Christ to others.

meditation

Finally, brothers, whatever is true, whatever is noble,
whatever is right, whatever is pure, whatever is lovely,
whatever is admirable—if anything is excellent or
praiseworthy—think about such things. Whatever you
have learned or received or heard from me, or seen in me—
put it into practice. And the God of peace will be with you.

PHILIPPIANS 4:8-9

session 3

can you commit?

Be devoted to one another in brotherly love. Honor one another above yourselves. Never be lacking in zeal, but keep your spiritual fervor, serving the Lord.

ROMANS 12:10-11

As a teenager, you undoubtedly experienced the high anxiety that goes along with that big rite of passage: the driver's license. When you are 15, everyone *except* you has their learner's permit and is on the road day and night with someone who will teach them what they need to know to pass the dreaded test. You are the only one left out! Until you have a driver's license, you're sure you are nothing, a social outcast destined to never go anywhere in life—literally! So you gotta have it *now*.

If this is so important, then why on earth do we heartless adults and the Department of Motor Vehicles operate in denial mode? Why do we require that teens have a license before they get behind the wheel? Simply this: We know how easy it is to be damaged or killed by driving a car. So an understanding of the rules of the road, a smattering of practice in a safe environment and the proof of commitment (that's insurance) are required before we say, "Okay. You're ready. Here's a license."

Sex isn't much different. To a teen, it seems as if he or she is the *only one* in the world who is still a virgin. It seems as if the only way to get respect as a full-fledged man or woman is to have sex. And of course, he or she needs to do it *now*.

But we heartless adults operate in denial about this too. Why? Because having a complete relationship is more dangerous than driving; it requires lots of risk taking. And we all know how easily damage can result if a complete relationship (the kind that includes sexual intercourse) isn't handled with the respect it deserves. So there's a license for this rite of passage too—a marriage license.

True, granting a couple a marriage license doesn't prove that either of them will be an enjoyable mate, a terrific sexual partner or even a person who regularly takes out the garbage. But for a Christian couple prepared by the Spirit of God and wise helpers, the marriage license signifies their understanding of the "rules of the road." They've probably gotten in some practice in relating. And most important, they're committed to the idea of staying together exclusively. Commitment is what will make them willing to work on taking out the garbage and each of them being a better mate. It's the license to have before two people get into a bed together.

Sex outside of marital commitment is only full of fear and anxiety.
We shouldn't give ourselves fully until we get a commitment.

LISA PELUSO, ACTRESS

group study guide

can you
commit?

starter

TAKE A STAND: Put signs that read "agree" and "disagree" on opposite walls of the room. Stand in the middle of the room and read each statement listed below aloud to the group, and then have each student stand on the side of the room that best describes his or her view. While they do not have to definitely choose one side or the other, they may not stand in the middle of the room. If appropriate for your group, ask for volunteers to explain their position on each statement.

1. If you are really in love, it's okay to have premarital sex.
2. If you're not ready for marriage, you're not ready for sexual intercourse.
3. Premarital sex bases a relationship on physical aspects.
4. If you're pretty sure you're going to get married to the person, premarital sex is okay.

Note: You can download this group study guide in 8$\frac{1}{2}$" x 11" format at
www.gospellight.com/uncommon/resisting_temptation.zip.

5. Premarital sex offers a false sense of intimacy.

6. People who have premarital sex are likely to cheat on their spouses after they are married.

7. Having premarital sex can have physical, emotional and psychological consequences.

8. Sex is the main way to show someone that you truly love him or her.

9. Couples—married or just dating—need to have sex to release sexual tension.

10. A person shows that he or she values and cares for you by having sex with you.

11. Having premarital sex will have an impact on your future relationships.

12. It's important to have sex before you are married to make sure you are sexually compatible.

message

First Corinthians 6 is the first of two letters written by Paul to the church in Corinth. The readers of these letters were Christians, but they weren't acting like Christians. The Bible says that our salvation does not depend on our actions, but that because of our faith in Jesus, our actions should reflect our faith. Paul wrote to the Corinthians to remind them of the importance of their actions; and in the second half of chapter 6 of the first Corinthian letter, Paul addressed the sexual activities the Corinthians were participating in.

Read the following passage from 1 Corinthians 6:12-20. As you read these verses, consider these questions: (1) How does God view our bodies and what we do with our bodies? (2) How is sexual sin different from other sins?

"Everything is permissible for me"— but not everything is benefi-cial. "Everything is permissible for me"—but I will not be mas-tered by anything. "Food for the stomach and the stomach for food"—but God will destroy them both. The body is not meant for sexual immorality, but for the Lord, and the Lord for the body. By his power God raised the Lord from the dead, and he will raise us also. Do you not know that your bodies are members of Christ himself? Shall I then take the members of Christ and unite them with a prostitute? Never! Do you not know that he who unites himself with a prostitute is one with her in body? For it is said, "The two will become one flesh." But he who unites himself with the Lord is one with him in spirit.

Flee from sexual immorality. All other sins a man commits are outside his body, but he who sins sexually sins against his own body. Do you not know that your body is a temple of the Holy Spirit, who is in you, whom you have received from God? You are not your own; you were bought at a price. Therefore honor God with your body.

dig

1. Verse 12 says, " 'Everything is permissible for me'—but not everything is beneficial." What does this mean?

   _____

   _____

   _____

   _____

   _____

   _____

   _____

2. How does this relate to our sexuality?

_____
_____
_____
_____
_____
_____
_____

3. How does this passage describe our bodies?

verse 13

_____
_____
_____
_____

verse 15

_____
_____
_____
_____

verse 19

_____
_____
_____
_____

4. Paul says that our bodies are a part of Christ (see verse 15) and have the Holy Spirit inside them (see verse 19). How should this knowledge impact our interactions with our boyfriend or girlfriend?

_____

_____

_____

_____

_____

5. Even though all sin is literally "missing the mark" and "falling short of God's glory" (see Romans 3:23), Paul points out in 1 Corinthians that sexual sin is different from other sins. In what way is sexual sin different from other sins?

_____

_____

_____

_____

_____

6. Read 1 Corinthians 6:19-20. Write these verses in your own words.

_____

_____

_____

_____

_____

7. How do these verses relate to your relationship with the opposite sex?

_____

_____

_____

_____

_____

_____

_____

8. What does "you [and your body] are not your own" mean?

_____

_____

_____

_____

_____

_____

9. According to verse 20, what's our response to be to Christ's love for us?

_____

_____

_____

_____

_____

_____

_____

apply

As Christians, we are to approach dating and relating to the opposite sex in a manner different from the world's. Why? Because we have the Holy Spirit of God dwelling inside of us. Imagine this conversation:

> *Tyler, you are not just dating Jill, who is beautiful, with a wonderful smile and a great personality; you are dating Jill who has the very Spirit of God dwelling inside of her. Honor her as you would any sister in Christ. Jill, you aren't just dating Tyler, this hunk of a guy with dreamy good looks and a great personality; you are also dating Tyler who has the Holy Spirit of God living inside of him. The Bible says to "outdo one another in showing honor" (Romans 12:10, RSV). You are called to radically respect each other.*

1. What does "radically respect each other" mean?

    _____

    _____

    _____

    _____

2. Showing you love someone by *not* having sex with him or her is counter to what the world tells us. What are some reasons for following God's recipe for love and not the world's?

    _____

    _____

    _____

    _____

    _____

3. Sex is one of many ways that married couples demonstrate
   their love for each other. But God is explicit that sex is to
   be saved for marriage. In spite of this, there are lots of
   other ways that unmarried couples can express their love
   for, appreciation of and commitment to each other. Brainstorm a few other ways that two people in a relationship
   can demonstrate their love in a way that is pleasing to God.

4. It is important to remember that sex is not bad. God created it for a husband and wife to enjoy each other. It is the
   temptation to have sex outside of God's intentions that is
   unhealthy. Just as food itself is not bad for you, but over-
   indulging in food can be bad for you, sex itself is a God-
   given gift, but sexual immorality (premarital sex, adultery,
   pornography and so forth) is not healthy. The challenge to
   you is to commit your sexuality to God and refrain from
   sexual intercourse until marriage. Why would this be a
   proper response to your commitment to God?

5. Many young people indicate their commitment to God to
    stay sexually pure by taking what is called "the Sexual Pu-
    rity Pledge." This pledge is as follows:

    *Believing that God's best for my life is to keep my life sexually pure
    and refrain from sexual intercourse until the day I enter mar-
    riage, I commit my body to God and my future mate.*

    How does this pledge honor God?

    _____

    _____

    _____

    _____

    _____

    _____

    _____

6. How does this pledge honor your current boyfriend or
    girlfriend?

    _____

    _____

    _____

    _____

    _____

    _____

    _____

7. How does it honor your future spouse?

_____

_____

_____

_____

_____

8. How does it honor your own body?

_____

_____

_____

_____

_____

Are you ready to make a commitment to be sexually pure? If so, sign and date the pledge below.

---

the purity code pledge

In honor of God, my family and my future spouse, I commit my life to sexual purity. This involves:

- Honoring God with my body.
- Renewing my mind for the good.
- Turning my eyes from worthless things.
- Guarding my heart above all else.[1]

_____   _____

signature   date

---

9. Congratulations! You just made a promise that will have life-long benefits for you, your faith, your body and your future spouse. But making any pledge—whether it is to raise your grades, to exercise more or to stay sexually pure—takes more than just lip service. It takes *action*. What actions will you take in order to stay true to your pledge?

    _____

    _____

    _____

    _____

10. A pledge is also strengthened when we have accountability. In the space below, write the name of two people who you will share your commitment with and who you will ask to hold you accountable.

    _____

    _____

11. The Bible acknowledges that we will be tested in our lives—this includes our goal for sexual purity. But God does not leave us alone in these challenges. Write in your own words the promises that the following verses hold:

    Romans 8:26-27

    _____

    _____

    _____

    _____

1 Corinthians 10:12-13

_____
_____
_____
_____
_____
_____

2 Corinthians 12:9-10

_____
_____
_____
_____
_____
_____

James 1:2-6

_____
_____
_____
_____
_____
_____

James 1:12

_____
_____
_____
_____
_____
_____

reflect

1. What helps people to refrain from sexual intercourse until marriage?

    _____

    _____

    _____

    _____

    _____

2. Is it realistic in today's culture to remain a virgin until marriage? Why or why not?

    _____

    _____

    _____

    _____

    _____

3. What one question about sex would you like to ask God?

    _____

    _____

    _____

    _____

    _____

4. Why did you decide to take or not take the Purity Code Pledge?

_____

_____

_____

_____

5. What will be the hardest part about keeping this pledge?

_____

_____

_____

_____

6. God is not going to strike you with a lightning bolt if you fail to live up to your pledge, but there will be consequences. What are some of these consequences?

_____

_____

_____

_____

meditation

Don't let anyone look down on you because you
are young, but set an example for the believers in speech,
in life, in love, in faith and in purity.

1 TIMOTHY 4:12

Note
1. Jim Burns, *The Purity Code* (Minneapolis, MN: Bethany House Publishers, 2008).

drawing the line

No temptation has seized you except what is common to man.
And God is faithful; he will not let you be tempted beyond what
you can bear. But when you are tempted, he will also provide
a way out so that you can stand up under it.

1 CORINTHIANS 10:13

Because God made us in His image both inside and out, He treats us with the respect due to a work of His creation. He not only sees us warts and all, but He also knows us deep inside. The person we think nobody knows is open before Him! And He values that inner person in each of us far more than even we do.

Satan, on the other hand, loves to foster *dis*respect: It's a usual vehicle for laughs in situation comedies. And it's defended in songs and movies as "standing your ground" and "respecting yourself," a kind of fierce self-protection that means everyone else better give way. And frankly, in our society, we admire this ruggedly individualistic mentality. But disrespect destroys relationship.

And we've learned that respect and relationship are what God seeks to build.

On this session's issue of deciding how far is too far, we can be assured that almost every young person has (consciously or unconsciously) already drawn some lines for him- or herself. But these lines may not be ones they will talk about readily: They know what they are supposed to say in church. For many teens, this is just another time to play the great charade, say the right words and get out as quickly as possible. Since you're teaching boundaries as a matter of respect, be sure to show your respect for the teens in your class. Don't pressure them into making a group or public effort on this subject if you suspect a lack of honesty. Your challenge is to find ways to give your teens a chance to think honestly about this issue—without pressuring them into saying what you want to hear. It's a matter of respect.

Temptation isn't always thrown at us on Make-Out Point. Today's key verse says simply that temptation is common; God is faithful; there's always a way out. As teachers, we may be tempted to pressure, to push, to be sure everybody says the right words. But remember that God is faithful. He respects you and the students you teach. He can make a way out of this temptation just as surely as He can keep your young people pure.

Can you please warn people about the dangers of going too far? I speak from experience that emotions get carried away, and you may say and make all the resolutions not to have sex but later it becomes a different story. . . . All the "in-between" needs to be addressed because it's what leads to sex.

TEENAGE GIRL

drawing the line

starter

THE RELATIONSHIP GRAPH: Friends who have sex . . . a couple who never talk about their feelings . . . a girlfriend who is more emotionally involved in the relationship than her boyfriend—all are lopsided relationships. A healthy relationship has balance. Balance ensures that all aspects of a relationship are in proportion to each other and that one element doesn't become more of a focus than others.[1]

Below are three different relationship situations. As a group, discuss each situation, and then determine the degree of commitment in each area listed in the chart. Place a dot at the intersection of the area of commitment listed of the left side of the graph and the percentage of commitment listed at the bottom of the graph.

1. Lucas and Maria have been dating for five weeks. Maria is a Christian, but she hasn't told Lucas because she is afraid that he won't like her as much. Maria really likes Lucas, but every

time they are together he pushes her to go farther physically than she is comfortable with or thinks is right. When they are together, Lucas likes to talk about himself and rarely asks Maria questions about herself. Since they've started dating, Maria spends most of her time with Lucas and rarely sees her friends much anymore. Lucas occasionally also goes out with Suzy, but he considers Maria his main girlfriend.

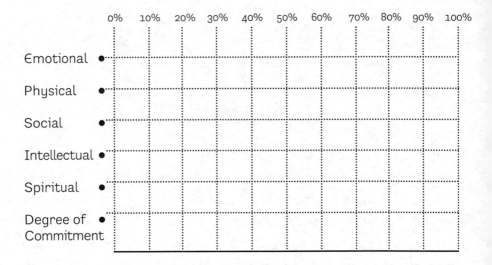

2. Tom and Cara have had a solid friendship for two years. They are active in the church youth group and really enjoy serving on the leadership team. Tom and Cara enjoy long hours of talking together about everything from spiritual life to music. Although they have known each other for a long time, they have just recently become boyfriend and girlfriend. Since becoming a couple, they've gone out to see a movie together and also visited an amusement park with mutual friends. Tom kissed Cara goodbye after the youth-group ski trip.

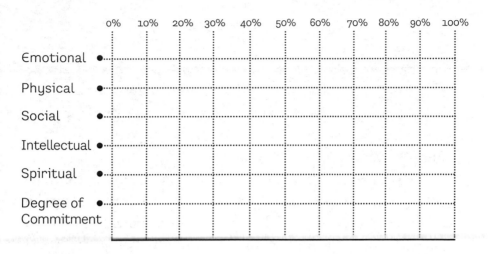

3. Anna and Eddie work together. Anna tells Eddie everything that is going on in her life. Eddie seems to be listening but rarely asks questions or tells Anna about himself. Anna is a touchy-feely person and is always giving Eddie hugs. She tells people that Eddie is her boyfriend, though they've never been out on an official date or discussed being a couple. Anna is a new Christian and would like to talk more about Jesus since Eddie is a leader in his church's youth group, but he doesn't talk about it much.

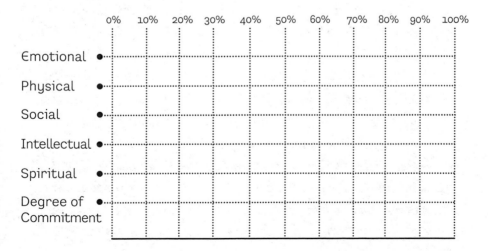

message

Finding the proper balance in a relationship is not easy, and determining an appropriate physical relationship is often one of the most tempting issues to tip the scale. Why are thinking about balance and boundaries in a relationship—especially in regard to your physical relationship—so important?

If you've ever sat down with a whole half gallon of ice cream and a spoon and thought, *I'll just take a bite,* or ever started up that computer game, thinking, *I'll only play for a few minutes,* you know that when we don't set boundaries for ourselves ahead of time, we often end up going much farther than we had intended.

The same is true of our physical relationship. But unlike having a stomachache or the tired, dull glaze of having wasted four hours on the computer, the consequences of going past a physical boundary can have a huge impact in our life.

First Thessalonians was written by Paul as a letter to new believers in Thessalonica who needed instruction and guidance on how to set boundaries and live godly lives. Read the following passage from 1 Thessalonians 4:1-8. As you read, consider the following questions: (1) What are the consequences of sexual immorality? (2) What kind of life has God called us to?

Finally, brothers, we instructed you how to live in order to please God, as in fact you are living. Now we ask you and urge you in the Lord Jesus to do this more and more. For you know what instructions we gave you by the authority of the Lord Jesus.

It is God's will that you should be sanctified: that you should avoid sexual immorality; that each of you should learn to control his own body in a way that is holy and honorable, not in passionate lust like the heathen, who do not know God; and that in this matter no one should wrong his brother or take advantage of him. The Lord will punish men for all such sins, as we have already told you and warned you. For God did not call us to be impure, but to live a holy life. Therefore, he who rejects this instruction does not reject man but God, who gives you his Holy Spirit.

dig

1. What does "be sanctified" mean (verse 3)?

2. Think about your current relationship or any relationship between a boyfriend and girlfriend. Practically, how can you "control [your] own body" in a way that is holy and honorable" (verse 3)?

3. If we allow lust and passion to override us, what are we like?

4. According to these verses, what are the consequences of sexual immorality?

    ----

5. Sometimes we think that our sins just impact us. We can forget that our sins can have consequences for other people too. How can your sexual sins impact other people?

    ----

6. God calls us to live holy lives. What does this mean in your own life? Are you living a holy life?

    ----

7. If God were here in the flesh, would you look Him in the eye and say, "God, I'm going to disobey You because I like my boyfriend [girlfriend] more than You." Most of you probably wouldn't dream of doing this. But the way that we act may be sending this very message to God. Do your

actions and behaviors with your boyfriend or girlfriend glorify God?

_____

_____

_____

_____

apply

The Sexual Purity Pledge in the last session required you to commit your sexuality to God and refrain from sexual intercourse until marriage. Does that mean that everything except sexual intercourse is fair game? Not exactly. Reread 1 Thessalonians 4:1-8.

1. In your own words, how does the Bible describe how we ought to act?

    _____

    _____

    _____

    _____

2   Notice how the Bible defines "sexual immorality":

    You should avoid sexual immorality; that each of you should learn to _____ his own _____ in a way that is _____ and _____, not in passionate _____ like the heathen, who do not know _____. For God did not call us to be _____, but to live a _____ life (verses 4-5,7).

3. In light of Paul's words in 1 Thessalonians 4:1-8, circle
    which of the following behaviors would be acceptable for
    you to engage in.

    Hugging   French kissing
    Holding hands   Oral sex
    Making out   Touching breasts/ genitals

4. So, exactly how far should you go? As the saying goes, the
    best offense is a good defense. By setting your boundaries
    before you are faced with crossing them, you provide your-
    self with a better chance of sticking to them. So let's think
    about it now.

    The chart below gives you an opportunity to catego-
    rize specific actions and determine the type of relation-
    ship in which each one belongs. Consider each of these
    actions in light of this question: What would be pleasing
    to God? And remember, God loves you and wants the very
    best for you. Note that the headings range from "Friends"
    to "Married."

    At the bottom is a list of abbreviations. Each letter(s)
    stands for a certain action. Write the letter(s) in the col-
    umn or columns representing the relationship in which
    you think that the action would be pleasing to God. For
    example, "SI" for "sexual intercourse" has already been
    placed in the "Marriage" column.

    We know God's will for intercourse. It is clearly set
    forth in the Bible. For the other listed actions, thought-
    fully and logically determine the standards that will be
    best for you and that will glorify God. (*Note:* Letters can be
    used multiple times.)

Friends	Dating	Exclusive Dating	Engaged	Married
				SI

L =   Looking at someone of the   SO = Touching sexual organs
      opposite sex   DH = Dry humping/motions of
HH = Holding hands when   sexual intercourse with
      together   clothes on
HG = Hugging   UN = Being in your underwear
K =   Light kissing   together
MK = Making out   NK = Being naked together
FK = French kissing   O =   Oral sex
B =   Touching the breasts   SI = Sexual intercourse

5. Sexual actions are meant to lead to sexual intercourse—
   one action progressing to another. When you come to the
   end of your limits, you are often tempted to go beyond

them. Read 1 Corinthians 10:13. What "way out" does
God provide for us in sexual temptation?

_____

_____

_____

_____

_____

Every normal red-blooded young person will most likely, at one
time or another, come in contact with sexual temptation—this includes Christian couples who are working to remain sexually
pure. Matthew 26:41 says, "Watch and pray so that you will not
fall into temptation. The spirit is willing, but the body is weak."
Even if our mind and spirit have decided one thing, often times,
in the moment, our bodies want to do something different. So
how can we make sure to keep our body in line with what our
mind and spirit have decided to do?

6. Think of some ways to avoid sexual temptation. Be cre-
    ative. The pull of sexual temptation can be strong, and
    you want to be prepared with an arsenal of tricks to help
    you stick to the plan you've set for yourself. Then share
    these suggestions with the group as a whole.

_____

_____

_____

_____

_____

7. Without God's help, let's face it: We're in trouble! Fortunately, God has a promise for us. Read Philippians 4:13. What promise does God give us?

_____

_____

_____

_____

_____

Here are six positive steps to overcoming sexual temptation:

1. *Talk about the problem with your boyfriend or girlfriend.* If you do not feel comfortable enough to talk with him or her about your problem, you are definitely going too far and need to seriously consider where your relationship is going to take you.

2. *Set standards.* As you get to know your special friend, talk about the standards you would like to set in your relationship. Don't be afraid your friend will think you are a prude. He or she will respect you; if not, is the relationship worth it? Set your standards before you find yourself in the wrong place at the wrong time.

3. *Have others hold you accountable.* Tell a close friend, a trusted adult and/or your youth-group leader about your commitment to stay sexually pure and avoid sexual temptation. Ask them to pray for your commitment and to check in with you occasionally to see how you are doing.

4. *Plan dates that are fun and enjoyable.* One way to overcome sexual temptation is to stay away from driving to Make-Out Point or lying in bed together. Plan dates that allow you to have a lot of fun, be around others and include time for good communication and getting to know more about each other.

5. *Let God be a part of your dating life.* Invite God on your dates. Let Him lead you and direct you to the right people to date. Many Christians find it a great help to pray before a date. This puts the date in a proper perspective and often will remind both of you that, in a very real sense, the Lord goes with you on your dates.

6. *Break up.* If you are unable to overcome sexual temptation, it would be wise to break up. At the time, you might not feel that there are other guys or girls out there, but there are; and there are some out there who are better for you. Also remember that a breakup does not have to mean forever. Perhaps both of you need some time to redirect your thoughts. At another point in your life, you may be able to get back together.

reflect

1. What is the hardest part about staying sexually pure?

_____

_____

_____

_____

_____

2. How is sexual temptation different from other kinds of temptation?

3. Linda is 14. She says she isn't planning on having sex before marriage, but believes doing anything else physical with her boyfriend is okay. What advice would you give her?

4. Think about your future husband or wife. How would you feel if you knew that your future spouse was engaging in sexual activities with another person? How might that impact your future relationship?

5. Why would God warn us about sexual immorality and set
   aside sexual intercourse for marriage?

   _____

   _____

   _____

   _____

   _____

6. Has this study changed your view of the importance of
   sexual purity or your definition of "sexual purity"? If so,
   in what ways?

   _____

   _____

   _____

   _____

   _____

meditation

Let your eyes look straight ahead, fix your gaze directly before you. Make level paths for your feet and take only ways
that are firm. Do not swerve to the right or the left; keep your
foot from evil. For a man's ways are in full view of the Lord.

PROVERBS 4:25-27; 5:21

Note
1. Chap Clark, *Next Time I Fall in Love* (Grand Rapids, MI: Zondervan, Youth Specialties, 1987),
   adapted from p. 104. Used by permission.

unit II

resisting the temptation of drugs and alcohol

Let me introduce to you Darlene. This beautiful girl is 14. She is active in church and school and is a good student. She is from a middle-class home, where she lives with both parents. By the time she graduates from high school, chances for her involvement with drugs and alcohol are pretty good:

- There is a 75 percent chance she will try alcohol
- There is a 44 percent chance she will try marijuana
- There is a 22 percent chance she will use marijuana regularly
- There is a 9 percent chance she will try cocaine
- There is a 28 percent chance she will become engaged in heavy drinking (more than 5 drinks within a couple of hours)

• There is a 10 percent chance that she will smoke cigarettes frequently (more than 20 days each month).[1]

It's not like it used to be when we were in junior and senior high school. Sure, we were 11, 13, 16 and 18, but we were never their age, were we? They experience so much at such an early age. The mistake some of us have made is that we believe only bad teens use drugs and abuse alcohol. Wrong. Most young people will try both drugs and alcohol, but the teens who develop a problem are the ones who don't understand the powerful affect of drugs and alcohol on their person.

why do teens abuse drugs and alcohol?

First off, although drugs and alcohol provide only a false sense of relief, most of the time they're used by teens to deaden a perceived pain. Second, drugs and alcohol are so appealing to students (and adults) because they work every time. Drugs and alcohol are dependable while family and friends are, unfortunately, not always dependable. If a young person is worried about family struggles, grades, loss of a boyfriend or girlfriend or some other problem, the drugs or alcohol can be counted on to make the hurt go away—at least temporarily. It's this simple: Drugs make teens feel good, and drugs work. These two facts are absolutely essential to understanding the incredible draw, by so many, toward harmful dependency and addiction.

what happens when teens use drugs and alcohol?

First, they stop learning how to cope properly with stress. At whatever age they started putting a chemical inside them to deaden their pain, they stopped learning how to cope properly with stress. It's easy to detox an alcoholic or a drug user. The more difficult part is to re-teach a user how to deal with his or her problems in a way that is different from drinking or using drugs.

Second, their behavior begins to change in recognizable stages. No one takes a drink of his or her first beer and instantly becomes addicted, so it's important for youth workers to know the stages or change in order to help with prevention:

stage 1: experimental
· the youth tries alcohol or experiments with drugs

stage 2: social use
· he or she moves to more regular use with a higher tolerance

stage 3: dependency
· at this stage, the alcohol or drug use often becomes a daily preoccupation
· the youth begins to use harder drugs and alcohol a higher number of times a week
· he or she begins to have subtle changes in behavior, such as a drop in school grades and evident laziness

stage 4: addiction (harmful dependency)
· the youth is preoccupied with getting high all the time
· he or she loses control in limiting alcohol or drug intake
· he or she violates personal value system
· he or she often moves from one peer group to another

Now, this is where you come into the picture. One of the most effective ways to help students with the issue of drug and alcohol abuse—besides good parenting—is educating teens and talking with them in your church's safe setting about this important part of their life. As you go through this unit of four sessions, you will, no doubt, have students at every stage of change and some who are just deciding what to do about their use of alcohol and drugs. During these sessions, you will have a good opportunity to help young people make wise decisions and prevent an incredible amount of pain in life by educating them about drugs and alcohol.

As you do this, keep in mind this Scripture: "Do you not know that your body is a temple of the Holy Spirit, who is in you, whom you have received from God? You are not your own; you were bought at a price. Therefore honor God with your body" (1 Corinthians 6:19-20).

You have the opportunity to educate, challenge and encourage teens to look at what they are doing to their temple when they put a negative substance into their body. You will help them see just how it affects their entire life—including their spiritual life.

Are you ready? Buckle you seat belt and hang on, because you may be in for a wild ride. And thanks for being there for your students. You may be the only significant adult they can talk to about this serious issue.

Note
1. Danice K. Eaton, PhD., Laura Kann, PhD, Steve Kinchen, et al, "Youth Risk Behavior Surveillance—United States, 2005," Department of Health and Human Services Center for Disease Control and Prevention, *Morbidity and Mortality Weekly Report*, June 9, 2006, vol. 55, no. SS-5.

drugs at your doorstep

Do you not know that your body is a temple of the Holy Spirit, who is in you,
whom you have received from God? You are not your own; you were bought
at a price. Therefore honor God with your body.

1 CORINTHIANS 6:19-20

Drug and alcohol use and abuse are not new; people have always had something available to them to help them forget their troubles. The days of the Whiskey Rebellion passed to the days of the hard-drinking Old West, which passed to the days of opium smoking in the 1890s. During the era of Prohibition, the availability of alcohol was an ironic joke. And then came the beginning days of prescription-drug abuse and the availability of heroin and marijuana, which preceded the psychedelic 1960s. Coping with life's problems by dropping out, turning on or tuning out has always been available in one form or another.

So why the big concern about drug and alcohol abuse today? The temptations aren't new. They're common. It's partly a matter of greater availability. It's also a matter of greater pressure. But the bottom line is this: Our students live and move in a society where adults (through everything from pop songs to movies, but mainly through personal example) are not teaching young people *any* methods of dealing with problems other than walking away, getting drunk or getting stoned.

Your challenge is not just to educate. It goes beyond exhorting teens to keep the temple of the Holy Spirit clean and usable. Even more vital is to prove—by your life—what having a body that is God's temple means. You must show—by your responses to problems—biblical ways of dealing with trouble. Then you'll really be helping your teens.

Once they understand the ways Christians can solve problems, when they see they have the resources to deal with trouble, when they know where they can go for real help—the world's shoddy methods of dealing with trouble and pain will be shown up for what they are: empty promises. Never forget what an effective method of teaching by example is: Jesus left us just such an example, which we should follow in His steps. Give your young people the gift of your example.

I don't consider [marijuana] a drug. It's a plant. Coke.
I don't do that. . . . That's a drug.
TEENAGE BOY

drugs at your doorstep

starter

ALCOHOL 101: Have the students divide into groups of three or four each. Read each of the following questions, and then have the students in the groups try to guess the correct answer. (You might want to put the questions on a PowerPoint slide that you can display on a screen.) Then, as a whole group, discuss the answers to the questions.

1. Heavy drinking of alcohol over a long time can cause damage to what?
   a. the brain
   b. the liver
   c. the heart
   d. a, b and c

2. The No. 1 drug problem among young people is what?
   a. crack
   b. alcohol
   c. tobacco

3. Which of the following has as much alcohol as 1 ounce of whiskey?
   a. 12 ounces of beer
   b. 8-ounce glass of wine
   c. 12-ounce wine cooler
   d. a, b and c

4. Which of the following statements are true and which ones are false?
   a. Alcoholism is the same as being drunk.
   b. A person who is an alcoholic can control his or her urge to drink.
   c. While drinking, people often say or do things they wouldn't normally say or do.
   d. Alcohol is a drug.
   e. Long-term alcohol abuse can shorten a person's life.
   f. A child of an alcoholic parent is less likely to abuse alcohol.

5. What are two ways alcohol affects the body?

   _____

   _____

   _____

   _____

   _____

6. What are two of the main reasons that young people
   drink alcohol?

   _____

   _____

   _____

   _____

   _____

Answers: (1) D. Alcohol can kill cells and weaken these organs. (2) B. More
than half of all junior and senior high school students have tried alcohol.
(3) D. Each has about the same amount of alcohol. (4a) **False.** A person can
drink and get drunk but not be an alcoholic. (4b) **False.** An alcoholic is not in
control of his or her drinking. (4c) **True.** As a person drinks more and more,
he or she loses control of some faculties. (4d) **True.** A drug is a psychoactive
substance that speeds up or slows down a person's body. Alcohol slows it
down. (4e) **True.** Long-term drinking can cause fatal diseases. (4f) **False.** Alcoholism tends to run in families. (5) Alcohol slows down a person's brain and
bodily control. (6) Peer pressure; to declare their independence; to have more
fun; to combat loneliness; to reduce anxiety and fear; and so on.

message

Some people believe that the Bible does not say anything specific
about drugs or alcohol, but God makes His intentions for how
we are to live and behave clear. As you go through this session,
consider the following questions: (1) What's wrong with using alcohol (and drugs)? How should we treat our bodies? Read each of
the Scripture passages below, and then summarize them in your
own words:

Woe to those who rise early in the morning to run after their drinks, who stay up late at night till they are inflamed with wine. They have harps and lyres at their banquets, tambourines and flutes and wine, but they have no regard for the deeds of the LORD, no respect for the work of his hands (Isaiah 5:11-12).

Let us behave decently, as in the daytime, not in orgies and drunkenness, not in sexual immorality and debauchery, not in dissension and jealousy. Rather, clothe yourselves with the Lord Jesus Christ, and do not think about how to gratify the desires of the sinful nature (Romans 13:13-14).

The acts of the sinful nature are obvious: sexual immorality, impurity and debauchery; idolatry and witchcraft; hatred, discord, jealousy, fits of rage, selfish ambition, dissensions, factions and envy; drunkenness, orgies, and the like. I warn you, as I did before, that those who live like this will not inherit the kingdom of God (Galatians 5:19-21).

Therefore do not be foolish, but understand what the Lord's will is. Do not get drunk on wine, which leads to debauchery. Instead, be filled with the Spirit. Speak to one another with psalms, hymns and spiritual songs. Sing and make music in your heart to the Lord (Ephesians 5:17-19).

_____

_____

_____

_____

_____

dig

1. According to each of these verses, what are the consequences of drunkenness?

    _____

    _____

    _____

    _____

    _____

2. Does the Bible prohibit the consumption of alcohol? What evidence from Scripture supports your conclusion?

    _____

    _____

    _____

    _____

    _____

3. Even if someone is of legal drinking age, why might obe-
   dience to God for some people mean that they abstain
   from alcohol?

   _____

   _____

   _____

   _____

   _____

   _____

4. What are the consequences that drugs and alcohol can
   have on . . .

   your health?

   _____

   _____

   _____

   your appearance?

   _____

   _____

   _____

   _____

   your mental/emotional state?

   _____

   _____

   _____

   _____

your relationship with your parents?

_____

_____

_____

_____

your relationship with God?

_____

_____

_____

your ability to share your faith with others?

_____

_____

_____

_____

5. The Bible is clear on how we ought to view, treat and use
   our bodies. God created us in His image (see Genesis 1:27)
   and tells us that our bodies are not our own (see 1 Corinthians 6:19-20). For each passage, write a brief summary of
   how or why we ought to honor God with our bodies.

   Romans 13:12-14

   _____

   _____

   _____

   _____

1 Corinthians 6:19-20

_____
_____
_____
_____

2 Corinthians 5:9-11

_____
_____
_____
_____

1 Thessalonians 5:7-9

_____
_____
_____
_____

1 Peter 1:12-14

_____
_____
_____
_____

6. Why is how we treat our bodies a way to bring glory to God?

_____
_____
_____
_____
_____

7. Is it possible to honor God with your body when you are
   drunk or high?

   _____

   _____

   _____

   _____

   _____

apply

1. Studies show that 75 percent of teens will try alcohol, 44
   percent will try marijuana, and 9 percent will try cocaine. In
   addition, 22 percent of teens will go on to use marijuana
   regularly, and 28 percent will become engaged in heavy
   drinking. Do these statistics surprise you? Why or why not?

   _____

   _____

   _____

   _____

   _____

2. These statistics are on a national level. How might they
   differ from the statistics for your school?

   _____

   _____

   _____

   _____

   _____

3. First Peter 5:8 states, "Be self-controlled and alert." Why might it be hard to follow this verse when you are under the influence of drugs or alcohol?

_____

_____

_____

_____

4. The second part of this verse says, "Your enemy the devil prowls around like a roaring lion looking for someone to devour." Why are you easier "prey" for the devil when you are under the influence of drugs or alcohol?

_____

_____

_____

_____

5. What are some reasons teens drink and do drugs? Write these reasons on the left. Then, on the right, write at least two alternative actions a person could take.

Reasons Teens Drink/Do Drugs	Alternate Actions
boredom	try out for a sport, learn an instrument

reflect

1. How prevalent a problem are drugs and alcohol at your school? At your church?

    _____

    _____

    _____

    _____

2. What are your fears for your friends who drink or use drugs?

    _____

    _____

    _____

    _____

3. Despite the fact that it is illegal, the use of alcohol and drugs by some teenagers continues. What are some ways to keep teens from drinking and doing drugs?

    _____

    _____

    _____

    _____

4. What do you think the impact of seeing Christian teens drinking or doing drugs is on non-Christians?

    _____

    _____

    _____

    _____

5. How would drinking or doing drugs impact your relation-
    ship with Jesus?

    _____

    _____

    _____

    _____

    _____

6. What are some good reasons *not* to drink or do drugs.

    _____

    _____

    _____

    _____

    _____

meditation

Therefore, I urge you, brothers, in view of God's mercy,
to offer your bodies as living sacrifices, holy and
pleasing to God—this is your spiritual act of worship.
Do not conform any longer to the pattern of this world,
but be transformed by the renewing of your mind.
Then you will be able to test and approve what God's will is—
his good, pleasing and perfect will.

ROMANS 12:1-2

the "feel-good" factor

If any of you lacks wisdom, he should ask God, who gives generously
to all without finding fault, and it will be given to him.

JAMES 1:5

As you are well aware, when you stand in front of teens for any length of time, they pick up on everything about you. They know what really gets to you, they know how sincere you are, and they probably know what your shoe size is.

Then the time comes when a young person needs to talk, and to this teen, you may well be the only adult a teen knows who seems open. But what will you say to the student who comes to you and wants to tell you about his or her drug or alcohol problem? Of course, the teen will already know whether you are really interested and available. (That was pegged the first time he or she sat in your class.) But he or she may be terrified of your response.

So what *is* a proper response? Are you going to turn the student in to the authorities? Tell his or her parents? How much confidentiality will you keep? Will you somehow give him or her the impression that it's okay to cover this up? Will you call in another counselor?

The answers aren't going to be provided here! There are no pat answers, because these aren't any pat questions. But what this does point out is the need for a *prayerful* reaction. Don't wait for that young person to take you by surprise. Start now to pray earnestly! Part of the challenge for you is to provide a safe place where teens who do need help can come without fear. Ask God to literally give you the facial expressions, the voice and the control you need to let a student talk freely.

Your job is not to condone, but you must listen without judging until the problem is all laid out. Why? Because your reaction is the first step in recovery for the teen who comes to you. He or she is already not handling life's problems well. Your response is a living lesson in how to deal with the problem the teen has revealed—no blowing up, giving up, turning on or getting drunk. You'll teach a great deal just by what you show.

You'll need God's help for proper reactions, wisdom and words. And He will give you all you need for this delicate task. Don't fail to ask Him!

> *The first time we tried the vocal on "Alcohol,"*
> *he was too drunk to sing it. That's rather poetic.*
> GIBBY HAYNES, MUSICIAN

the "feel-good" factor

starter

FEELING GOOD: Have students complete the sentences. Then, as a whole group, have volunteers share some of their responses.

1. My perfect day—a day that would make me the happiest and that would make me feel my best—would be . . .

_____

_____

_____

_____

2. I feel good physically when . . .

_____

_____

_____

_____

3. I feel good mentally when . . .

4. I feel good spiritually when . . .

5. Three things that help me feel better when I'm low are . . .

6. I get the most joy in my life from . . .

message

Everyone wants to feel good about themselves. And we try all sorts of things to try to accomplish this feeling. We do things we like, buy things we like, spend time with people we like. And let's be frank: Drugs and alcohol can make you feel good—at least for a while. But that feeling isn't true joy, and it doesn't last.

The Bible shows us examples of people searching for the "feel-good" feeling too. In Ecclesiastes 2, the writer struggles with the question of what brings true joy and true fulfillment in life—the real "feel-good" feeling. The passage at times seems contradictory, but remember that we are seeing the writer's thoughts as he is trying to figure out what matters in life and what can bring true joy.

Read the following passage in Ecclesiastes 2:1-11,17-25. As you read these verses, consider the following questions: (1) What kinds of things does the writer try to find fulfillment in? (2) What does the writer conclude at the end of the passage?

I thought in my heart, "Come now, I will test you with pleasure to find out what is good." But that also proved to be meaningless. "Laughter," I said, "is foolish. And what does pleasure accomplish?" I tried cheering myself with wine, and embracing folly—my mind still guiding me with wisdom. I wanted to see what was worthwhile for men to do under heaven during the few days of their lives.

I undertook great projects: I built houses for myself and planted vineyards. I made gardens and parks and planted all kinds of fruit trees in them. I made reservoirs to water groves of flourishing trees. I bought male and female slaves and had other slaves who were born in my house. I also owned more herds and flocks than anyone in Jerusalem before me. I amassed silver and gold for myself, and the treasure of kings and provinces. I acquired

men and women singers, and a harem as well—the delights of the
heart of man. I became greater by far than anyone in Jerusalem
before me. In all this my wisdom stayed with me.

> *I denied myself nothing my eyes desired;*
> *I refused my heart no pleasure.*
> *My heart took delight in all my work,*
> *and this was the reward for all my labor.*
> *Yet when I surveyed all that my hands had done*
> *and what I had toiled to achieve,*
> *everything was meaningless, a chasing after the wind;*
> *nothing was gained under the sun. . . .*

So I hated life, because the work that is done under the sun was
grievous to me. All of it is meaningless, a chasing after the wind. I
hated all the things I had toiled for under the sun, because I must
leave them to the one who comes after me. And who knows
whether he will be a wise man or a fool? Yet he will have control
over all the work into which I have poured my effort and skill un-
der the sun. This too is meaningless. So my heart began to despair
over all my toilsome labor under the sun. For a man may do his
work with wisdom, knowledge and skill, and then he must leave
all he owns to someone who has not worked for it. This too is
meaningless and a great misfortune. What does a man get for all
the toil and anxious striving with which he labors under the sun?
All his days his work is pain and grief; even at night his mind does
not rest. This too is meaningless.

A man can do nothing better than to eat and drink and find
satisfaction in his work. This too, I see, is from the hand of God, for
without him, who can eat or find enjoyment? To the man who
pleases him, God gives wisdom, knowledge and happiness, but to

the sinner he gives the task of gathering and storing up wealth to
hand it over to the one who pleases God. This too is meaningless, a
chasing after the wind.

dig

1. What things does the writer try in an attempt to find out
    "what was worthwhile for men to do under heaven during
    the few days of their lives" (verse 3)?

    _____

    _____

    _____

    _____

2. What was the effect of the writer's attempting to cheer him-
    self with wine (see verse 3)?

    _____

    _____

    _____

    _____

3. According to verse 11, what does the writer realize about
    all of his attempts to feel good?

    _____

    _____

    _____

    _____

4. Can you relate to the writer's feelings? What would be included on your list of things you thought would make you feel good but ultimately didn't?

    _____

    _____

    _____

    _____

    _____

5. What does the writer conclude at the end of the passage?

    _____

    _____

    _____

    _____

6. So what does this passage have to say about using drugs and alcohol to make us feel good—whether it is just for fun or to forget a problem? Is this an effective solution? Is it a godly solution?

    _____

    _____

    _____

    _____

    _____

Remember that when you use drugs or alcohol, you are actually destroying nerve receptors in your brain, which can cause you to become forgetful, slow your thinking process, and at times blunt or deaden your emotions so that you don't feel pain. But just because you may not be experiencing the pain doesn't mean that the pain has gone away. The pain still exists.

True joy, fulfilling happiness and the real "feel-good" feeling can only come through Jesus. The high from drugs and alcohol will wear off. Friends will disappoint. Life will let you down. But Jesus promises this: "Surely I am with you always, to the very end of the age" (Matthew 28:20).

apply

1. Is someone who uses drugs or alcohol every once in a while any better in God's eyes than someone who uses frequently? Why or why not?

_____

_____

_____

_____

2. When people start using drugs and alcohol, they tend to change in four stages:

   Stage 1: Experimental Stage. They may make comments such as, "Just one sip"; "I'll only get high this once"; or "What's the big deal?"

   Stage 2: Social Use. This leads to regular use with an increased tolerance.

   Stage 3: Dependency. This includes a daily preoccupation with drugs or alcohol, the use of harder drugs and alcohol, a higher usage per week and changes in behavior, such as getting lazy and letting grades drop.

Stage 4: Addiction. This includes a preoccupation with getting high, a loss of control, violation of personal value system and moving from one peer group to another.

What does "slippery slope" mean?

_____

_____

_____

_____

_____

3. Have you seen examples in your friends or in your own life of how drugs and alcohol use can be a slippery slope? What was the result?

_____

_____

_____

_____

_____

4. Is it possible to keep yourself from moving from one stage of change to the next? Why or why not?

_____

_____

_____

_____

_____

5. Besides the fact it is illegal to use drugs and illegal for those
    under age to use alcohol, what is the problem with using
    drugs or alcohol to forget a problem or deaden a pain?

    _____

    _____

    _____

    _____

6. At whatever age people start relying on drugs or alcohol to
    deaden their pain, that is the age at which they quit coping
    with stress properly. Using drugs and alcohol can have both
    short-term and long-term impacts. Read the following sce-
    narios, and then think about the short-term and long-term
    consequence that might result from each situation.

    Scenario 1: *You are having a horrible day. So many things have
    gone wrong that it's almost funny. Almost. A friend invites you
    over to hang out at his house with some mutual friends of yours.
    His parents are gone and suddenly someone pulls out a bottle of
    booze. You don't normally drink, but you've had such a bad day,
    you decide to take a sip—and then another and another until you
    are light-headed and doing karaoke on the living-room table.
    You've forgotten all about your bad day, but you've also forgotten
    where you put your wallet and are starting to feel a bit queasy.*

    What are the potential short-term consequences?

    _____

    _____

    _____

    _____

What are the potential long-term consequences?

Scenario 2: *All your hard work has paid off and, as a freshmen, you are on the varsity basketball team. After practice, some of your teammates decide to hang out behind the locker room to smoke a joint someone stole from his brother. You want to be accepted by your older teammates and stay behind with them. When the joint gets passed to you, the coach suddenly comes around the corner. Everyone runs and you are left alone, holding the joint.*

What are the potential short-term consequences?

What are the potential long-term consequences?

Scenario 3: *It's only your third date with him, but he's taken you up to "Make-Out Point" to watch the sun go down. You love spending time with him, and he always does romantic things to make you feel special. This time he has brought along some chocolate-covered strawberries and a bottle of his parent's wine. You have reservations about drinking, but you really like this guy and don't want to lose him. After you have just a few sips, you notice that he has finished his first cup and has poured himself another.*

What are the potential short-term consequences?

_____

_____

_____

_____

What are the potential long-term consequences?

_____

_____

_____

_____

7. Drugs and alcohol can seem like a quick fix to a problem, but as we've talked about, neither is truly a solution. What are some creative ideas that *don't* involve drugs or alcohol for dealing with or solving the following problems?

Your boyfriend or girlfriend broke up with you

_____

_____

_____

_____

Your parents have been fighting or have gotten a divorce

_____

_____

_____

_____

You're feeling bad about yourself

_____

_____

_____

_____

You don't have anything to do on a Friday night with your friends

_____

_____

_____

_____

reflect

1. Habits can begin unintentionally but, once set, are hard to break. What is your habit for dealing with a problem in your life? Is this a healthy way to deal with problems?

_____

_____

_____

_____

2. How does a low self-image relate to drug and alcohol use?

    _____

    _____

    _____

    _____

3. If you saw a friend having problems with drugs or alcohol,
    how would you intervene and help?

    _____

    _____

    _____

    _____

4. Why are drugs and alcohol a dangerous "solution"?

    _____

    _____

    _____

    _____

5. Think of some famous people or others you know (with-
    out using their names) who have crashed and burned be-
    cause of drug or alcohol use and abuse. How did drugs or
    alcohol affect their careers, relationships and health?

    _____

    _____

    _____

    _____

6. How is your faith impacted when you rely on drugs and alcohol to cope with your problems?

_____

_____

_____

_____

_____

_____

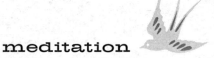

meditation

"I have set the Lord always before me;
Because He is at my right hand I shall not be moved.
Therefore my heart is glad, and my glory rejoices;
My flesh also will rest in hope.
You will show me the path of life;
In Your presence is fullness of joy;
At Your right hand are pleasures forevermore."

PSALM 16:8-9,11, *NKJV*

the fight for control

"For I know the plans I have for you," declares the LORD, "plans to prosper you and not to harm you, plans to give you hope and a future."

JEREMIAH 29:11

Some young people are aiming for the top: He wants to play professional basketball. She wants to become a gymnast. These teens know what discipline is about. They've sacrificed to gain the goal they are seeking. These teens usually have already said no to drugs and alcohol simply because the use of those things would keep them from their goal of peak physical performance.

But maybe you don't have a group of motivated athletes before you. Maybe they're just normal students who like to do a lot of things but don't have a driving ambition for physical perfection. What can you tell them about balancing their lives and disciplining themselves to avoid the use of drugs and alcohol?

Drug and alcohol use is a symptom. If a teen feels as if he or she isn't going anywhere in life, isn't driven and motivated by something, drug and alcohol use can end boredom, make a person feel better and certainly motivate someone—although not to desirable behavior!

So what's the answer? A comprehensive physical fitness program? No. We have the very best motivator, the kind that can spur students on to self-discipline. It's the antidote to boredom, to aimlessness, to feeling as if they aren't going anywhere. And it's just this simple: When young people begin to understand that *God* thinks they are important and wants to see them be all that He has made them to be, when they realize that He has *important* plans for each of them, then discipline—saying no—begins to make sense.

Share with your students the wonder and excitement of the big plans God has for each of their lives. And don't keep this on the theoretical level. Tell them about the exciting ways God has revealed His plans for your life and the lives of others right around you. God always has something infinitely better than the glitter Satan flashes before our eyes. Give your teens the vision of their amazing value to God, His big plans for each of them, and the excitement of knowing what He is up to!

The only discipline that lasts is self-discipline.
BUM PHILLIPS

the fight for control

starter

THE BALLOON TRIBE: Divide the class into three groups. (If the three groups are too large, you can divide the class into six or nine groups.) Give each student a copy of "The Balloon Tribe" story on the following page, or use a PowerPoint slide to display a copy onscreen. Read aloud the story, and then assign a position to each group. At the end of the story, the groups will defend their positions.[1]

Group 1: Blowing up balloons is fine, and it's okay to run out of breath and get dizzy if you feel like it.

Group 2: Occasional balloon blowing is okay, but it's morally wrong to get dizzy.

Group 3: Blowing up balloons is wrong at all times and a person should never do it.

Note: You can download this group study guide in 8½" x 11" format at **www.gospellight.com/uncommon/resisting_temptation.zip.**

the balloon blowers

There is a primitive tribe with a unique social activity. This is the story of how that activity originated and the effects it had on the tribe.

It seems that a short while back, one of the tribe members discovered a stretchy substance that came from a local tree. At first, the tribe didn't think this discovery was very important. However, from that substance one tribe member was able to invent what we know as a balloon. The tribe thought it a clever but seemingly useless invention.

One day, however, that same tribe member discovered something interesting about the balloons. After blowing up several of them, he became lightheaded and out of breath, experiencing a euphoric, dizzy feeling. When he told this to the rest of the tribe, everyone immediately wanted to try it. Eventually, as this activity increased, the tribe became divided into four groups: The Dizzy Balloon Blowers, the Occasional Balloon Blowers, the Balloon Blowers for Career or Craft, and the Anti-Balloon Blowers.

The Dizzy Balloon Blowers developed a tolerance for blowing up several large balloons in a short time—usually in just one evening. They would get together every week and blow up numerous balloons for different reasons. Some would do it to get dizzier than the time before; some as just a reason to get together with their friends; some because it was a way to relax after a hard day in the jungle; some to celebrate; and some because they weren't getting along with other tribe members. Each tribe member felt that his or her reason for blowing up balloons was worth it, though all of them often felt sick and nauseated in the morning.

The Occasional Balloon Blowers enjoyed a balloon every once in a while. In fact, when they did join the Dizzy group, they would take up a whole evening blowing up just one balloon (which was usually not too large). These tribe members blew up balloons for all the same reasons as the Dizzy group but were careful to avoid having to go through what the Dizzies went through the morning after.

The Balloon Blowers for Career or Craft turned balloon blowing into an art. They only blew up the best balloons, not just any old cheap balloon. In fact, many of this group made their own balloons. And fine balloons they were! It was not long after balloons were discovered that this group started contests and competitions to find the best balloon. They examined each balloon's shape, size and color and how well it expanded. Many in this group got very good at making balloons and did so full-time.

On the other side of the jungle were the Anti-Balloon Blowers. They had seen the effects from blowing up too many balloons and loudly protested that absolutely no one should blow up balloons! The Anti-Balloon Blowers said balloon blowing had caused tribe families to break up and hate one another. They argued that many tribe members had given up their tribal responsibilities so that they could blow up balloons all day and get dizzy.

With the many groups of balloon blowers and the Anti-Balloon Blowers, it was difficult to assess the overall benefit or detriment of balloon blowing on the tribe. Some members would not touch balloons while some seemingly could not face life without them. Every tribe member had to make up his or her own mind about what to do with the balloons.

message

Self-control is not an easy trait to possess, and the lack of it can have a profound impact on us. Though some people may innately possess more self-control than others, for most of us, it is a quality that takes work, perseverance and, most importantly, God. Read the following passage in Romans 8:5-8,12-14. As you read, consider the following: (1) What is the result of living by our sinful nature? (2) How do we break free from our sinful nature?

> *Those who live according to the sinful nature have their minds set on what that nature desires; but those who live in accordance with the Spirit have their minds set on what the Spirit desires. The mind of sinful man is death, but the mind controlled by the Spirit is life and peace; the sinful mind is hostile to God. It does not submit to God's law, nor can it do so. Those controlled by the sinful nature cannot please God. . . . Therefore, brothers, we have an obligation—but it is not to the sinful nature, to live according to it. For if you live according to the sinful nature, you will die; but if by the Spirit you put to death the misdeeds of the body, you will live, because those who are led by the Spirit of God are sons of God.*

dig

1. Define "self-control."

   ----

2. What is the "sinful nature" this passage talks about?

    _____

    _____

    _____

    _____

3. According to this passage, is it possible to follow the sinful nature and God?

    _____

    _____

    _____

    _____

4. We cannot follow two paths at the same time. Jesus says that no one "can serve two masters" (Luke 16:13). And our actions often speak louder than our words. Are your words and actions matching up? What are the consequences of letting the sinful nature gain control of your life?

    _____

    _____

    _____

    _____

5. What does "led by the Spirit" mean (verse 14)?

    _____

    _____

    _____

    _____

6. Do you think that most teenagers are in control of their
    drinking and/or drug use?

    _____

    _____

    _____

    _____

    _____

    _____

7. Read Galatians 5:16-18. Notice that this verse does not
    say, "If you try really hard to have a lot of self-control, you
    will not gratify the desires of the sinful nature." It also
    doesn't say, "If you generally are a good person, you will
    not gratify the desires of the sinful nature." According to
    these verses, what is the only way to avoid fulfilling the de-
    sires of the sinful nature?

    _____

    _____

    _____

    _____

    _____

    _____

8. Later in Galatians, self-control is listed as one of the fruits
    of the Spirit: "But the fruit of the Spirit is love, joy, peace,
    patience, kindness, goodness, faithfulness, gentleness and
    self-control. Against such things there is no law" (5:22-23,
    emphasis added). The only way to truly win the battle over
    our sinful nature is by living by the Spirit, and the Spirit

will give us the tools and traits that we need to be victori-
ous in times of temptation. Read the following verses. Why
should self-control be an important aspect of our faith?

2 Corinthians 5:9-11

---

1 Thessalonians 5:7-9

---

1 Peter 1:13-15

---

2 Peter 1:5-9

apply

1. Suppose you believe you have pretty strong self-control. Tonight you plan to go to a party, where you'll just have one drink and then stop. How can using drugs or alcohol affect the amount of self-control you have?

    _____

    _____

    _____

    _____

2. Though some instances like driving a car too fast or eating candy and soda every day provide clear feedback to your senses that things aren't right, drugs or alcohol are substances that dull your receptors and slow down your thinking and reasoning processes. So, how would a person know if he or she had passed the point of being in control?

    _____

    _____

    _____

    _____

3. What is your impact on non-Christians when they see you lose self-control in regard to using drugs and alcohol?

    _____

    _____

    _____

    _____

4. You may be tempted to believe it is okay to use drugs or alcohol with your Christian friends because those friends know the "real" you. They know the "real" you doesn't normally act like that or say those kinds of things, and deep down they know you still love Jesus. So, what is the harm of using drugs or alcohol with your Christian friends?

_____

_____

_____

_____

_____

5. Read Galatians 6:1-10. What does this passage say about drug and alcohol use within a group of Christian friends?

_____

_____

_____

_____

_____

6. "Just Say No" was a slogan for the government's anti-drug campaign from 1980 to 1990, but its message is still relevant and still clear today: If someone offers you drugs or alcohol, just say no. It really can be that simple. But sometimes it can help to have other techniques (humor, distractions, alternatives) to turn down offers of drugs and alcohol. Read through the following situations, and then write down one or two realistic short refusals for each specific circumstance.

Situation 1: *Your sister and her friend pick you up from a party, and her friend offers you a cold beer for the trip home. (One possible answer could be, "You don't want to give me an open bottle in a moving car. I'm a total klutz and will spill it everywhere.")*

_____

_____

_____

_____

Situation 2: *At the skate park, a friend pulls out some bottles of cough syrup. She promises that if you drink one, you will feel as though you are in another world.*

_____

_____

_____

_____

Situation 3: *You miss the bus and an attractive senior offers you a ride home in her car. She takes a bag of white powder and stashes it in the glove compartment. She says she has nothing to do that afternoon and asks if you are interested in trying some of the new crack she just bought.*

_____

_____

_____

_____

Situation 4: *Your parents take you out to a nice dinner at a local club. Your dad orders everyone something to drink and tells you that it's okay for you to have one.*

_____

_____

_____

_____

_____

_____

Situation 5: *Between classes, you head to the bathroom. Someone from your soccer team walks in, lights up a joint and asks if you want a hit.*

_____

_____

_____

_____

_____

_____

Situation 6: *At a party, the gang gets into the parents' liquor cabinet. Everyone starts drinking out of a bottle of vodka and passing it around the room. Suddenly the bottle is in front of you.*

_____

_____

_____

_____

_____

reflect

1. What is your personal philosophy and guidelines for drug and alcohol use? Are your philosophy and guidelines consistent with your faith?

_____

_____

_____

_____

_____

2. Should you attend a party where you know drugs and drinking will be prevalent? Why or why not?

_____

_____

_____

_____

3. Self-control can affect all areas of our lives—from what we eat and say to how we act and respond. In what areas of your life is it hardest to maintain self-control?

_____

_____

_____

_____

4. Should a Christian drink socially? Where would you draw the line?

5. Do you want to have self-control? Do you want to keep your sinful nature from ruling your life? Why or why not?

6. What are some techniques that you use for maintaining your self-control?

7. Have you ever lost your self-control? What were the consequences? How did you feel?

8. A Japanese proverb states, "First the man takes a drink;
    then the drink takes a drink; then the drink takes the man."
    Write your own wisdom about avoiding the control of
    drugs and alcohol.

    _____

    _____

    _____

    _____

    _____

meditation

Be self-controlled and alert. Your enemy the devil prowls
around like a roaring lion looking for someone to devour.
Resist him, standing firm in the faith, because you know
that your brothers throughout the world are
undergoing the same kind of sufferings.

1 PETER 5:8-9

Note
1. Larry A. Dunn, *Ideas Number Thirty-Seven* (Grand Rapids, MI: Zondervan, Youth Specialties, 1985), pp. 30-31. Used by permission.

substance abuse involving friends or family

Do not love the world or anything in the world. If anyone loves the world, the love of the Father is not in him. For everything in the world—the cravings of sinful man, the lust of his eyes and the boasting of what he has and does—comes not from the Father but from the world. The world and its desires pass away, but the man who does the will of God lives forever.

1 JOHN 2:15-17

Recently making the rounds was a cartoon showing a large convention hall with a banner hung across the front: Welcome Children of Normal Parents. Seated in the vast hall was an audience of three people!

Now you may have had truly normal parents. But many people have felt at one time or another that their upbringing *wasn't* normal. The term "dysfunctional" has become a buzzword often used to excuse someone's problems instead of bringing an under-standing of solutions. The example of having an elephant in your living room is an effective place to begin.

As you read through this lesson, stop to ask yourself, *What was the elephant in my parents' living room? What's the elephant in my living room?* Your "elephant" may not be substance abuse but some-thing more common, such as addiction to anger or manipulation of others through guilt. An honest consideration of these ques-tions may not make you comfortable! It can be a humbling expe-rience. But only when you're ready to go on your own elephant hunt can you fully appreciate what a humbling effort it may take for someone in your group who needs to help his or her own fam-ily or close friends.

The goal here is not to turn the class into a group therapy ses-sion or to turn your young people into a bunch of amateur psy-chologists. But don't be afraid of a show of emotions. Make it your goal to help your students understand that we are all sin-ners. We are all dysfunctional! The most important thing they can learn by understanding the problems of dysfunctional people (that's all of us) is that God is always bigger than any problem we can concoct and bigger than any family style that has crippled us. As they learn to define problems, teach them to bring the prob-lems before the Lord. Help them understand that as they pray earnestly, listen to God and obey Him, they can be part of His big plan to help someone else come into freedom from *whatever* ad-diction is holding him or her.

If you want me back, you've got to clean yourself up.

SIXTEEN-YEAR-OLD GIRL
(ADDRESSING HER CRACK-ADDICTED MOTHER)

substance abuse involving friends or family

starter

THE FAMILY SCULPTURE: Build a family sculpture that demonstrates the roles various family members assume. As you help volunteers assume various parts, explain why each person is placed as he or she is.

1. Father (addict): Stand Father on a chair in the front of the group. He is the focus of the family, the key figure.

2. Mother (enabler): Stand Mother next to Father. He should lean on her and put some of his weight on her so she feels the pressure of his addiction. She may get upset and throw away his drugs or alcohol, but she will continue to enable him.

3. Hero (child): Hero helps Mother support Father. He or she should have one arm on both parents. Hero does it all: he or she takes care of Mother and Father, is active in the church youth group, works a job to help the family, and gets all *As* in school. Hero wants Father to be proud; Mother calls on Hero for support.

4. Lost Child (child): Lost Child stands with his or her face against the wall. Lost Child withdraws from the family. Much of the family conversation is about Lost Child's attitude and actions. Lost Child leaves the home early and spends little time in communication with the family.

5. Clown (child): Clown walks around the family and tickles them. Clown hurts like everyone else but deals with the hurt by laughing it off.

6. Scapegoat (child): Scapegoat walks around the family and karate chops everyone. Scapegoat takes the focus off Father. Scapegoat often gets attention by copying Father's behavior of using drugs or alcohol.

As a whole group, discuss the following questions:

1. What would your life be like and how would you feel if you were . . .

Father?

_____

_____

_____

_____

Mother?

_____

_____

_____

Hero?

_____

_____

_____

Lost Child?

_____

_____

_____

Clown?

_____

_____

_____

_____

Scapegoat?

_____

_____

_____

_____

2. Do you have friends or family members who are living out some of these roles? How are they doing this?

_____

_____

_____

_____

_____

_____

_____

message

When our friends and family members abuse drugs and alcohol, the consequences can be ugly. We can be the victim of their out-of-control behavior and/or verbal attacks. We can see them destroying those things that are good in their lives. We can be left to pick up the pieces.

But Jesus' message is clear: "A new command I give you: Love one another. As I have loved you, so you must love one another. By this all men will know that you are my disciples, if you love one another" (John 13:34-35). Jesus calls us to the incredible task of showing love to everyone—friend or foe, family member or stranger, sober person or addict.

The book of Luke includes the story of "the good Samaritan," which demonstrates the kind of love God calls us to have for one another. Read the following passage in Luke 10:30-37. As you read, consider the following questions: (1) Why is it strange that the first two men passed the man without helping? (*Note:* A Levite was a member of the tribe of Levi and was designated as an assistant to the Temple priests.) (2) To what lengths did the Samaritan go to help the injured man?

> *In reply Jesus said: "A man was going down from Jerusalem to Jericho, when he fell into the hands of robbers. They stripped him of his clothes, beat him and went away, leaving him half dead. A priest happened to be going down the same road, and when he saw the man, he passed by on the other side. So too, a Levite, when he came to the place and saw him, passed by on the other side. But a Samaritan, as he traveled, came where the man was; and when he saw him, he took pity on him. He went to him and bandaged his wounds, pouring on oil and wine. Then he put the man on his own donkey, took him to an inn and took care of him. The next day he took out two silver coins and gave them to the innkeeper. 'Look after him,' he said, 'and when I return, I will reimburse you for any extra expense you may have.'*
>
> *"Which of these three do you think was a neighbor to the man who fell into the hands of robbers?"*
>
> *The expert in the law replied, "The one who had mercy on him."*
> *Jesus told him, "Go and do likewise."*

dig

If you're familiar with the story of the Good Samaritan, you'll remember that Jews and Samaritans did not like each other. In fact, Jews were so disgusted with Samaritans that they would walk hundreds of miles out of their way so that they wouldn't have to walk through Samaria. But in this story, it is the Samaritan man who goes out of his way and spends his time and money to help an injured Jewish man.

1. The Bible is full of verses that remind us that we need to help those in need. But the story of the Samaritan goes even further. What lesson can we take away from this story about helping others?

_____

_____

_____

_____

2. Why is it strange that both the priest and the Levite passed the injured man by, not only ignoring him, but also actually walking on the other side of the street to get farther away from him?

_____

_____

_____

_____

3. What steps did the Samaritan take to help the injured man?

_____

_____

_____

_____

_____

4. Describe the Samaritan's attitude about helping the injured Jewish man.

_____

_____

_____

_____

5. How can we relate this passage to loving friends or family members who are dealing with drug or alcohol abuse?

_____

_____

_____

_____

6. In the final verse of the passage, Jesus commands His listeners to go and show mercy in the same way that the Samaritan did. What is mercy?

_____

_____

_____

_____

7. What would showing mercy to a friend or family member struggling with substance abuse look like? What actions would show mercy?

_____

_____

_____

_____

apply

Assume for a moment that you have a friend named Sean. Sean is a great person. He is doing well as a pitcher on the varsity baseball team and is well liked by his peers. Sean's funny personality makes him popular, and others think of him as the class clown. Lately, however, you've smelled alcohol on Sean's breath and heard rumors that he has been using marijuana.

So far, Sean's athletic abilities haven't been affected. His grades have slipped a little, but he definitely isn't flunking out. As one of Sean's best friends, you've noticed some subtle changes in his behavior. He's not as friendly when he has beer on his breath. In fact, sometimes he can be downright mean. He is also getting a little freer with his language, and he hangs out with girls who are known for sleeping around. You know it's been a hard year for him, because his mom and alcoholic dad finally split up after several really rough years together.

1. What are all the issues affecting Sean's life?

2. What can you do to be a good friend to Sean?

3. What advice would you give Sean about his actions?

Now assume you have a friend named Laura. Laura tells you that she suspects her brother Mike is doing drugs. Though they used to practically be best friends, Laura and Mike have fallen away from each other and aren't as close as they used to be. Laura doesn't feel like she can say anything to him. "It's just a phase. I'm sure everything will work out fine," Laura says.

4. As Laura's friend, what advice would you give her?

5. What steps could Laura take to help her brother?

6. What are some ways or techniques you could use to start a conversation with a friend or family member about his or her substance abuse?

7. Keep in mind that you can't force a person to stop using drugs or alcohol. The decision must be his or her own. So, what can you do to help a person with a drug or alcohol problem? Brainstorm a list of steps you could take to help a friend or family member dealing with substance abuse.

_____

_____

_____

_____

_____

_____

reflect

1. If you were to notice that a friend or family member was having a problem with drugs or alcohol, what would the natural tendency be to do?

   a. Back off the friendship
   b. Confront the issues
   c. Do nothing, as long as it didn't affect you
   d. Preach at him or her
   e. Encourage him or her to get some help
   f. Other:

   _____

   _____

   _____

   _____

2. Have you ever had to confront a friend or family member with a substance abuse problem? What did you say?

_____

_____

_____

_____

3. What are the risks in confronting someone about his or her substance abuse problem?

_____

_____

_____

_____

4. What are the risks in *not* confronting someone who has a substance abuse problem?

_____

_____

_____

_____

5. Would it be easier for you to confront a Christian friend or a non-Christian friend? Why?

_____

_____

_____

_____

6. If you were struggling with drugs and alcohol, do you have friends or family members in your life who would be there to intervene?

_____

_____

_____

_____

_____

7. Do you currently have someone in your life who you think (or know) is struggling with drugs or alcohol? List three actions that you could take to try to help that person.

_____

_____

_____

_____

_____

meditation

God is our refuge and strength,
an ever-present help in trouble.

PSALM 46:1

unit III

resisting temptation from the media

Today's young people are part of a media-bombarded generation. If it's not music, then it's movies. If it's not movies, then it's magazines. If it's not magazines, then it's the good ole TV. Robert Pittman, former president and chief executive director of MTV, once said, "Early on we made a key decision that we would be the voice of young America. . . . We were building more than just a channel; we were building a culture."[1] Music expert Al Menconi believes that today's music aimed at teens (rock, rap, hip-hop and so forth) is effective because it meets three of youth's basic needs:

1. The rock star (via compact discs, videos and downloads) spends huge amounts of time with young people—providing them with companionship.

2. The rock star accepts young people as they are—providing them with acceptance.
3. The rock star relates to the problems of young people—providing them with identification.[2]

Fulfilling the need of companionship, acceptance and identification is all a part of youth ministry. Is it possible that the secular rock culture has done a better job in these areas than many parents and youth workers?

At times, I've been criticized for talking about today's secular music by some who say, "Stick to the Bible." Well, that's true—that's exactly what I and others interested in the health of our young people do. We need to help our young generation learn to discern what kind of "stuff" they are putting in their minds and how it subtly, or not so subtly, affects them. And the way we do that is through the Word.

The apostle Paul gave some great advice when he wrote, "Finally, brothers, whatever is true, whatever is noble, whatever is right, whatever is pure, whatever is lovely, whatever is admirable—if anything is excellent or praiseworthy—think about such things. Whatever you have learned or received or heard from me, or seen in me—put it into practice. And the God of peace will be with you" (Philippians 4:8-9).

Our job in the four sessions of this third unit is to help teens see the powerful influence of music and the media on their lives and to help teens develop a Christian approach to their listening and viewing habits. Let's not underestimate the facts:

1. Secular music is here to stay.
2. Most teens listen to several hours of secular music each day.

3. Music and the media *do* influence our teens to a greater extent than we realize.
4. Many of the "heroes" of secular music have lifestyles and philosophies that are opposed to God.
5. Most young people have not really thought from a Christian viewpoint about the music and media that are influencing their lives.
6. Young people will listen to you and are interested in how music does or does not influence them spiritually, as long as the presentation is done with grace and understanding.

With these points in mind, I pray that you have great sessions on discussing the media, one of young people's most influential and, perhaps, most controversial subjects. You're making a difference by bringing up issues like this. God bless you!

Notes
1. Robert Pittman, "The Man Behind the Monster," *Los Angeles Times,* July 28, 1991. http://articles.la times.com/1991-07-28/entertainment/ca-436_1_mtv-ne (accessed July 11, 2009).
2. Al Menconi, *Should My Child Listen to Rock Music?* (Elgin, IL: Life Journey Books, 1991).

gigo (garbage in, garbage out)

Finally, brothers, whatever is true, whatever is noble, whatever is right, whatever is pure, whatever is lovely, whatever is admirable—if anything is excellent or praiseworthy—think about such things.

PHILIPPIANS 4:8

Let's talk about the power of music for a minute. Think back to the days when you were a teen. Which popular songs do you still remember the lyrics to? (Some of us would have to confess to knowing more lyrics than Bible verses!) What songs had a kind of power in your life or changed your mind about something?

Music springs from the heart. And because of this, it involves us emotionally as we identify with the feelings of the singer or lyricist. Then we acknowledge or reject the content of the lyrics. But the desire to identify with the singer or lyricist can be so strong that even though our conscience doesn't agree with the content of the lyrics or we know that the lyrics aren't true or meant for our wellbeing, we just sing along anyway. And that active participation in the song reinforces the false ideas in our mind.

Those lyric phrases seem so neat, so adult, so well turned when you're a young person groping to understand love and relationships, truth and justice. "Don't get mad, get even"; "Love the one you're with"; "Only the good die young"—the list is endless and the truths are few. But those errors in thinking are often very nicely put. In fact, Satan must have a whole poetry division working overtime!

Music is far too powerful to be treated as casually as we do. It's never value-neutral because it's a cry of the heart. The question is, Whose heart is doing the crying out? Whose heart will we follow? Help your students practice using the "filter test" given by God in Philippians 4:8. After they've practiced this in class, encourage them to try using the test just for a week—at home, in the car, with friends. Encourage them to rewrite the lyrics of songs for themselves, to actually reflect and clarify what they believe. And let them know that it's okay to write their own lyrics! If God has put new songs in their heart, they don't have to sing along with the lies of the world any longer.

Wearing a dress shows I can be as feminine as I want. I'm a heterosexual . . . big deal. But if I were a homosexual, it wouldn't matter either.
Kurt Cobain (1967-1994), Musician

gigo (garbage in, garbage out)

starter

FILL ME UP: Have students individually choose the kinds of things that they are filling themselves up with. Point out that they should choose all the answers that apply. Do this activity yourself to describe your own habits.

1. The kind of food I eat most often can be described as . . .

    ☐ healthy
    ☐ grown in the ground
    ☐ fresh
    ☐ balanced
    ☐ energy-producing
    ☐ unvaried

    ☐ sugary
    ☐ out of a box, bag or jar
    ☐ salty
    ☐ from a fast-food place
    ☐ feel-good-producing
    ☐ highs/lows-producing

2. The kind of music I listen to most . . .

☐ is positive   ☐ is negative
☐ is uplifting   ☐ involves dark topics
☐ is glorifying to God   ☐ focuses on the bad in life
☐ is motivating   ☐ is destructive
☐ encourages me   ☐ depresses me
☐ positively portrays   ☐ includes negative or
     love and life   inappropriate language

3. The kind of movies and TV shows I watch most often . . .

☐ are educational or   ☐ provide a mental
     informational   escape from real life
☐ portray positive exam-   ☐ contain scenes of
     ples of relationships   premarital sex
☐ provide realistic   ☐ are filled with
     portrayals of life   violence
☐ are encouraging   ☐ contain foul language
☐ contain positive   ☐ use crass and distasteful
     messages   humor
☐ make me smarter   ☐ are mind-numbing

4. The books and magazines I spend the most time reading . . .

☐ are informational   ☐ are escape-oriented
☐ deepen my faith   ☐ lower my self-esteem
☐ provide positive stories   ☐ are trashy or gossipy
☐ are pleasing to God   ☐ are unpleasing to God
☐ are beneficial to some   ☐ make me want to buy
     part of my life   things I don't need

5. The kind of websites I spend the most time on . . .

☐ are school-related   ☐ are pornographic
☐ help keep me connected   ☐ are complete time-wasters
☐ have a positive influence   ☐ tend to be gossip sites
☐ are pleasing to God   ☐ give me the "wants"
☐ give me energy   ☐ keep me from doing tasks
☐ help me to learn new   ☐ make me feel bad about
   things   myself

message

What are you filling yourself up with? As the saying goes, "Garbage in, garbage out." If you fill your mind and body with garbage, you shouldn't be surprised when garbage comes out through your words, actions, outlooks and attitudes. The Bible says, "A man reaps what he sows" (Galatians 6:7). So what are you sowing in your mind? In your heart? In your life?

The world is constantly bombarding us with messages—many of which are not constructive. For most of us, a conscious effort is needed to discern whether or not we are consuming sounds, images and experiences that are beneficial for us. And we all—Christians new and old—can benefit from being reminded to look at what we are filling our minds with.

At the end of the book of Philippians, Paul's letter to the church in Philippi, Paul wrote about this very topic and urged the Philippians to keep focusing their lives on those things that would bring glory to God. Read the following passage in Philippians 4:4-9. As you read, consider the following questions: (1) What advice does Paul give to the Christians in Philippi? (2) What is the result of thinking about "such things" (verse 8)?

Rejoice in the Lord always. I will say it again: Rejoice! Let your gentleness be evident to all. The Lord is near. Do not be anxious about anything, but in everything, by prayer and petition, with thanksgiving, present your requests to God. And the peace of God, which transcends all understanding, will guard your hearts and your minds in Christ Jesus.

Finally, brothers, whatever is true, whatever is noble, whatever is right, whatever is pure, whatever is lovely, whatever is admirable—if anything is excellent or praiseworthy—think about such things. Whatever you have learned or received or heard from me, or seen in me—put it into practice. And the God of peace will be with you.

dig

1. What are some of the pieces of advice Paul gives to the Philippians in verses 4-6?

   ---

2. Is it easy for you to "not be anxious about anything" but to "present your requests to God" (verse 6)? How do you deal with difficult times?

   ---

3. Read Philippians 4:8 again. Do you think that you currently live this verse out in your life? Why or why not?

    _____

    _____

    _____

4. If we think about things that are pure, true and admirable, what will occur?

    _____

    _____

    _____

5. God is clear: Your mind matters to Him, and you have to be proactive in keeping your mind pure and staying. How do you do this? You keep away from negative influences, and you constantly renew your mind. Read Proverbs 13:20 and 14:7. What are some common negative influences?

    _____

    _____

    _____

    _____

    _____

6. Why are people drawn to negative influences, even when they know that those influences are bad for them?

    _____

    _____

    _____

7. Read Romans 12:2 and Colossians 3:1-4. How can we con-
    stantly renew our mind?

    _____

    _____

    _____

    _____

    _____

8. What does "set your minds on things above" mean?

    _____

    _____

    _____

    _____

apply

1. Do you think that it is important to consider the things
    that you see, hear and read?

    _____

    _____

    _____

    _____

    _____

2. How can your choices in what you read, watch and listen
    to impact your faith? Your attitude? Your actions?

    _____

    _____

    _____

    _____

3. Think about good things. For each phrase, list one example of something you could read, hear, see or do that possesses this quality.

Whatever is true . . .

_____

_____

_____

_____

_____

Whatever is noble . . .

_____

_____

_____

_____

Whatever is right . . .

_____

_____

_____

_____

Whatever is pure . . .

_____

_____

_____

_____

Whatever is lovely . . .

_____

_____

_____

_____

_____

Whatever is admirable . . .

_____

_____

_____

_____

_____

Whatever is excellent or praiseworthy . . .

_____

_____

_____

_____

_____

4. Why is it so hard to fill our minds with things that are pleasing to God?

_____

_____

_____

_____

_____

5. How does the message of Philippians 4:8 match with . . .

the music that you listen to?

_____

_____

_____

_____

_____

the TV shows and movies that you watch?

_____

_____

_____

_____

the books or magazines that you read?

_____

_____

_____

_____

_____

the online sites that you visit?

_____

_____

_____

_____

6. Read through the following scenarios, and then write what you would say to each person.

Scenario 1: *Your 12-year-old brother, Seth, has recently started listening to certain kinds of rap music with lyrics that condone drug and alcohol use, excuse violence against other people and portray women in a derogatory manner. What would you say to him?*

_____

_____

_____

_____

Scenario 2: *Your mom is addicted to watching* The Real Housewives of Orange County. *She closely follows all the drama and participates in a number of blogs about the show. You often hear her comment about what nice clothes, cars and jewelry all the women have. What would you say to her?*

_____

_____

_____

_____

Scenario 3: *Your best friend is consumed with celebrity gossip and constantly surfs websites and blogs to hear the latest news, see the newest fashions and follow the star trends. You've noticed that she's been complaining that she's fat, even though she is in great shape, and has said some underage stars who have been in the*

news for their misbehavior "really aren't that bad." What would
you say to her?

_____

_____

_____

_____

reflect

1. Why does God want our minds to be pure?

    _____

    _____

    _____

    _____

2. What can you do to purify your mind?

    _____

    _____

    _____

    _____

3. Look again at the starter activity. Is there one area where
    you struggle the most to please God with your decisions?

    _____

    _____

    _____

    _____

4. Think of some examples of people you know or celebrities
    you've heard about who live out the "garbage in, garbage
    out" lifestyle. Without using names, describe them below.

    _____

    _____

    _____

    _____

5. Spend a few minutes in individual prayer for an awareness
    of negative influences in your life. Write out a short prayer
    asking God's protection over your mind.

    _____

    _____

    _____

    _____

meditation

Let us throw off everything that hinders and the sin
that so easily entangles, and let us run with perseverance
the race marked out for us. Let us fix our eyes on Jesus, the
author and perfecter of our faith, who for the joy set before
him endured the cross, scorning its shame, and sat down
at the right hand of the throne of God.

HEBREWS 12:1-2

session 10

rock reality

Now choose life, so that you and your children may live
and that you may love the LORD your God, listen to his voice,
and hold fast to him. For the LORD is your life.

DEUTERONOMY 30:19-20

Before the advent of printing, live performances circulated popular music from one person to the next. During the Renaissance, printed copies of popular music were published for the first time, and sheets of paper called "broadsides" passed from hand to hand. But, due to many inventions and innovations in the past 100 years (the gramophone, radio, MTV, the Internet), the circulation of popular music has speeded up considerably. And in whatever form music is passed around, every generation can probably point to a song or two that has been "theirs," setting that generation apart from others.

As a generation grows up, it seeks its own identity, to be different from the last generation. Changes in pastimes, fashions and music are the most visible ways we older folks notice this growth. Until the dissolution of society as we know it, popular music is not going to go away. The classics aren't going to suddenly take over that spot marked for popular music in every teen's heart. As Neil Young has sung so often, "Rock and roll will never die." A lot of young people are banking on that for their identification.

The trouble is, of course, that song lyrics send messages. And they are often messages that we'd rather our students did not hear and certainly did not espouse. The world's philosophies about life's most important issues—love, respect, honesty and so forth—are often dead wrong. Set to music, these philosophies become singable lyrics, repeatable and, therefore, even more memorable. It's not so much that we are afraid that our teens will take to heart some rocker's admonition to kill their parents or commit suicide (though such lyrics should not be lightly dismissed); our teens can usually spot those blatant messages and recognize their worthlessness. The twisted philosophies in songs, however, are often much more subtle than that, and they can be truly destructive.

We talked earlier about the fact that Satan loves to destroy relationships. Help your young people to focus on the ways relationships are dealt with by popular music, be it rap, hip-hop, country western, rock 'n' roll or something else. Help your students understand that even while they identify with their generation, they are also members of another generation—God's chosen generation. They don't have to believe everything they hear.

They're expecting someone who's treading water to save them. . . .
I can barely keep myself together.
EDDIE VEDER, MUSICIAN

rock reality

starter

TAKE A STAND: Put signs that read "Agree" and "Disagree" on op-posite walls of the room. Stand in the middle of the room and read aloud each statement. Students should stand on the side of the room that best describes their view. While they do not have to definitely choose one side or the other, they may not stand in the middle of the room. If appropriate for your group, ask for volun-teers to explain their position on each statement.

1. The music you listen to doesn't really have that big of an impact on your life.
2. Listening to Christian music can have a positive impact on your faith.
3. The majority of secular musicians are moral people.
4. It's okay to listen to secular music as long as you don't lis-ten to the lyrics.

Note: You can download this group study guide in 8¹/₂" x 11" format at www.gospellight.com/uncommon/resisting_temptation.zip.

5. It is impossible to be a strong Christian and listen to secular music.
6. Secular music can have a positive effect on our lives.
7. Listening to secular music can create poor relationships with family and friends.
8. Some secular music lyrics have an important message for our generation.
9. Some secular musicians or groups are definitely anti-God in their words and lifestyle.

message

What kind of music do you like? Pop with a dash of country? Rhythm and blues with an occasional detour into rap? Classic rock nourished by a hidden love of classical?

For many of us, music is an important element of life. Music can move us, inspire us, affirm us and challenge us. It can remind us of who we are or who we want to become. It can be a solace in pain or a partner in celebration. What does music mean to you? Perhaps more importantly, what does the music that you listen to say to you? What messages are you constantly filling your mind with by the songs you listen to? What do your listening choices say to those around you?

Read the following passage in 1 John 2:1-6,15-17. As you read, consider the following questions: (1) What is the evidence that we know Jesus? (2) How do these verses relate to the music that we listen to?

My dear children, I write this to you so that you will not sin. But if anybody does sin, we have one who speaks to the Father in our de-

fense—*Jesus Christ, the Righteous One. He is the atoning sacrifice for our sins, and not only for ours but also for the sins of the whole world.*

We know that we have come to know him if we obey his commands. The man who says, "I know him," but does not do what he commands is a liar, and the truth is not in him. But if anyone obeys his word, God's love is truly made complete in him. This is how we know we are in him: Whoever claims to live in him must walk as Jesus did. . . .

Do not love the world or anything in the world. If anyone loves the world, the love of the Father is not in him. For everything in the world—the cravings of sinful man, the lust of his eyes and the boasting of what he has and does—comes not from the Father but from the world. The world and its desires pass away, but the man who does the will of God lives forever.

dig

1. According to this Scripture, what evidence in your life will demonstrate that you know Jesus?

   _____

   _____

   _____

   _____

   _____

Notice the point made in verse 4: The person who merely says, "I know Jesus; I am a Christian" but does not obey God's commands is called out as a liar. It is our *actions* that demonstrate our faith, not our words.

2. What does "walk as Jesus did" mean (verse 6)?

    _____

    _____

    _____

    _____

    _____

3. How can you relate verse 6 to the kind of music that you
    listen to?

    _____

    _____

    _____

    _____

    _____

4. Reread verse 15. In your own words, write down what this
    verse means. Share your answer with the group.

    _____

    _____

    _____

    _____

    _____

5. Some people take this verse to mean that we should not
    love our parents, our friends, music, the nature around
    us or even our bodies. Why keep the oceans clean? Why
    eat healthy or care about our friends? The Bible says not
    to love the world. In one sense this is true. We shouldn't
    love anything more than God. If we had to choose money,
    music, our friends or even our family over God, He calls
    us to choose Him above all else. But God made our bod-

ies. God made nature. God inspires people to create beautiful music. God desires us to have healthy relationships. And He commands us to take care of the things He has given to us, to honor Him with our bodies and to be good stewards of the earth. Read verse 16 again. How does this verse clarify what "the world or anything in the world" means (verse 15)?

_____

_____

_____

_____

_____

6. We are called not to love anything that is not from God—worldly things; things that come from our sinful, fallen nature; things that do not bring glory to God. How does this relate to the kind of music you listen to?

_____

_____

_____

_____

_____

7. Can secular music bring glory to God? Why or why not?

_____

_____

_____

_____

_____

apply

1. What are two of your favorite songs right now?

2. What do you like most about those two songs? The music? The lyrics? The "feeling" of each song? The dance moves from the video? The artist's lifestyle?

3. What do you know about the artist's lifestyle? His or her morals? His or her behavior? His or her beliefs?

4. Is it important to know these things about the artists and groups that you listen to? Why or why not?

5. How would you feeling listening to these songs with . . .

   a younger sibling, cousin or friend in the room?

   _____
   _____
   _____
   _____
   _____

   your parents in the room?

   _____
   _____
   _____
   _____
   _____

   God in the room?

   _____
   _____
   _____
   _____
   _____

6. List 4 to 5 popular songs in the left-hand column of the chart on the following page. After listing each song, place a check mark under each of the themes in the table that apply to that particular song.[1] Do you think it's possible to frequently listen to one kind of music or artist without listening to the words?

Violence				
Self-Abuse				
Rebellion				
Prejudice				
Perverted Sex				
Permissive Sex				
People as Objects				
Occult/Satanism				
Materialism				
Hedonism				
Gloom/Despair				
Escape				
Death				
Crude Language				
Anti-God				
Anti-Authority				
Anger/Agression				
Anarchy				
Alcohol/Drugs				
Song Title				

7. If you believe you can separate the music from the words, what happens when other people (for example, your friends, your parents or your siblings) hear you listening to this kind of music? What will they think?

    ....

    ....

    ....

    ....

8. Imagine for a moment that you are the music director at a new radio station, KGOD 97.9 FM. As director, you are responsible for choosing the songs to be played on your station. What programming guidelines could the following Scriptures help you to establish?

    James 4:4-8

    ....

    ....

    ....

    ....

    1 Peter 2:9-12

    ....

    ....

    ....

    ....

    1 John 2:15-17

    ....

    ....

    ....

    ....

1 John 4:1-5

_____

_____

_____

_____

9. The station's tagline is "good music, great artists, God-pleasing." Based on this, what kinds of factors should you consider when determining whether or not to play a certain musical artist?

_____

_____

_____

_____

10. Based on the factors you came up with in the previous questions, now make a list of some of the popular groups that you would play or not play.

Play	Do Not Play

reflect

1. How do you use music? To relax? To zone out? To pump up? To put words and melodies to your feelings?

2. How does music influence you? How big a part does secular music play in your life? How many hours a day do you listen to it?

4. What do you think Jesus would say about secular music?

5. What role does God currently play in your music-listening habits? Do you feel that you need to change your habits?

6. Do you think the beat of the music can have sexual or violent influences in a person's life? Why or why not?

_____

_____

_____

_____

7. What musicians or groups today are a positive influence on our minds and actions?

_____

_____

_____

_____

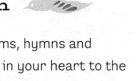

meditation

Speak to one another with psalms, hymns and
spiritual songs. Sing and make music in your heart to the
Lord, always giving thanks to God the Father for everything,
in the name of our Lord Jesus Christ.

EPHESIANS 5:19-20

Note

1. David Lynn, *Rock Talk* (Grand Rapids, MI: Zondervan, Youth Specialties, 1991), p. 31. Used by permission.

contemporary Christian music

Let the word of Christ dwell in you richly as you teach and admonish one another with all wisdom, and as you sing psalms, hymns and spiritual songs with gratitude in your hearts to God.

COLOSSIANS 3:16

You might unthinkingly hum a song all day, eventually realizing that it was the last thing you heard before you turned off the radio in the morning. God seems to have made our memories that way, for we seem to have a capacity for carrying a song around with us nearly all the time.

Of course, we believers are told in Colossians 3 that as Christ's word dwells in us, we will sing and make melody in our hearts to the Lord—a spontaneous response of grateful hearts and minds that are dwelling on God. And judging by the flood of new music available that praises and honors the Lord, many people are sharing the songs of their hearts!

Now some may object to contemporary Christian music. It's okay to prefer hymns or cantatas or oratorios. But remember these were once contemporary Christian music, too. (For instance, the tune for the Thanksgiving hymn "We Gather Together" was originally a bar song about a girl named Matilda.) Tunes and song styles for songs of praise to God have often come from popular music simply because it was singable and familiar, the musical vernacular of that particular generation.

We may not like every song style that comes down the pike, but, as we've seen, it's the content of the lyrics that is the key element. And although we need to be discerning (some songs that purport to be Christian are weak in content), we can be thankful that there are a wealth of songs in many styles to which we can sing along with free hearts and clear consciences. There's no spiritual merit in one song style over another!

And just as we talked about the importance of every generation finding its own identification, so also must every generation of believers find their own songs with which to praise God, to make His truth their own. As we drop our prejudices and let our own hearts sing for joy to God, we will find the grace to plug some patience in our ears and let our students crank up the volume to praise God. If it's not our style, so much the better!

When you take God and absolute morals out of society, then people will believe anything. And that's worse than believing nothing.
WES KING, CHRISTIAN MUSICIAN

contemporary Christian music

starter

SING A SONG: Divide students into groups of three or four each. Assign each group the tune of a well-known song (such as "Happy Birthday," a top-40 hit, "Mary Had a Little Lamb," and so forth). Have students write new lyrics about your youth group to go along with the tune and then perform the new lyrics for the whole group.

message

Do you have a favorite worship song? Why do you like it? How do you feel when it comes on the radio or is sung during a church service? Music can play a big role in our spiritual life. Music can quiet our mind, direct our attention, elevate our worship and excite our enthusiasm. Some people think that this kind of worship music is only for Sundays. But with contemporary Christian music, the joys of positive, motivating and worshipful music can be experienced every day.

Is some secular music positive and motivating? Absolutely. But when you listen to contemporary Christian music, you hear music that contains not only positive words but also messages that remind us of our need for God, that encourage us to be who we want to be in Christ and that direct our praise to the Creator of the universe. And our praise is something that God never tires of.

Read the following passage in Psalm 150. As you read, consider the following questions: (1) Is there a "right" or "correct" way to give praise to God? (2) What does God deserve praise and glory for?

> *Praise the LORD.*
> *Praise God in his sanctuary;*
> *praise him in his mighty heavens.*
> *Praise him for his acts of power;*
> *praise him for his surpassing greatness.*
> *Praise him with the sounding of the trumpet,*
> *praise him with the harp and lyre,*
> *praise him with tambourine and dancing,*
> *praise him with the strings and flute,*
> *praise him with the clash of cymbals,*
> *praise him with resounding cymbals.*
> *Let everything that has breath praise the LORD.*
> *Praise the LORD.*

dig

1. Although Psalm 150 was written thousands of years ago, its message still applies today. Think about the world you live in today. What are we to praise God for?

    _____

    _____

    _____

    _____

    _____

2. Read 1 Peter 4:12-14. What else does the Bible say that we ought to praise God for?

    _____

    _____

    _____

    _____

    _____

3. We may not have a harp or a lyre lying around, but based on Psalm 150, how can we apply what we ought to use to praise God?

    _____

    _____

    _____

    _____

    _____

4. In what situations are we to praise God?

5. In what situations do you find it hardest to praise God?

6. In what settings are we to praise God?

7. What other guidelines does this Scripture give for praising God?

8. Does contemporary Christian music meet these guide-
    lines? Why or why not?

    _____

    _____

    _____

    _____

    _____

    _____

    _____

apply

1. Complete the following sentences:

    Christian music is . . .

    _____

    _____

    _____

    _____

    _____

    _____

    I choose/don't choose to listen to Christian music because . . .

    _____

    _____

    _____

    _____

    _____

2. How many Christian groups or artists can you name?

3. What is one new Christian artist or group that you have heard recently that you enjoyed?

4. Where can you buy Christian music? List your favorite stores or websites for buying Christian music.

5. Are you interested in integrating more Christian music into your listening habits? Why or why not?

6. Do you think that listening to more Christian music might be beneficial for you? If so, what would the benefits be?

reflect

1. If you could meet any Christian or secular musician, who would you want to meet, and why?

2. In what ways are Christian musicians different from secular musicians? In what ways are they the same?

3. Could contemporary Christian music ever be a negative influence? If so, in what ways?

4. Are there any Christian bands or artists that you admire? What about them is admirable?

5. Imagine that you're a huge fan of a Christian band called For Him. You've downloaded all of their songs and have been to three of their concerts. Then you learn that the lead singer, Josh, had an affair while on tour. How would you respond to the news? Would you still purchase the band's music and attend their concerts?

6. How important to God is the kind of music you listen to? Why is it important to Him?

_____

_____

_____

_____

_____

_____

meditation

It is good to praise the Lord
and make music to your name, O Most High,
to proclaim your love in the morning
and your faithfulness at night,
to the music of the ten-stringed lyre
and the melody of the harp.
For you make me glad by your deeds, O Lord;
I sing for joy at the works of your hands.

PSALM 92:1-4

discretionary viewing

For the grace of God that brings salvation has appeared to all men.
It teaches us to say "No" to ungodliness and worldly passions, and to live
self-controlled, upright and godly lives in this present age.

TITUS 2:11-12

We all know young people who complain about having nothing to do because they've been trained to think that entertainment, not contribution, is their domain. Bored students get into trouble; drugs and alcohol are the quickest and easiest fix for boredom. The teens might not buy guns and shoot up their schoolmates, but if one picture is worth a thousand words and we see as much violence as pundits tell us we do, then it certainly is only the grace of God that keeps any of us from shooting everyone we know!

There's an interesting passage in Isaiah 33 that describes the person who can stand up during a time of judgment in Israel.

This person is described not only as one "who walks righteously," but also as one "who stops his ears against plots of murder and shuts his eyes against contemplating evil" (Isaiah 33:15). Imagine the effect that rule alone would have on our film and TV program selection! We so often think that what we see on TV or at the movies won't affect us because "it's not real." But do our minds know that? Can enough watching of others' demeaning, cruel, violent actions finally convince us that this behavior is acceptable? Ask your teens some questions that will reveal their attitudes toward other people. What about people who hurt them? Who hurt their family? Who hurt their friends? Listen for the subtle attitude shifts that indicate that the students have bought into the philosophies put forth on film. Like it or not, people on film are modeling behavior for all of us. And as we learned earlier, modeling is the most powerful kind of teaching possible.

Maybe it's an outrageous idea, but how about each of us grown-ups taking a *media* purity pledge? Would that cramp our styles too much, make us feel a little too far removed from "the real world"? Perhaps. But unless we begin by *our* modeling to show young people that what they are seeing on the big or small screen is less exciting than the real life God has for us, we're just talking. And remember that just *one* picture is worth a thousand words.

Lesbians. Homosexuals. Transvestites. Spiritualists.
Occultists. Teenage runaways. Teenage drug addicts. Teenage alcoholics.
Child stars who are in trouble.

ADULT FEMALE
(LISTING PEOPLE SHE HAS MET THROUGH TV PROGRAMS)

group study guide

discretionary viewing

starter

FAVORITES: Have students list three of their favorite websites, TV shows, and movies in the space below.

Three favorite websites that you visit most often:

1. _____
2. _____
3. _____

Three favorite TV shows:

1. _____
2. _____
3. _____

Three favorite movies:

1. _____

2. _____

3. _____

Now read Philippians 4:8: "Finally, brothers, whatever is true, whatever is noble, whatever is right, whatever is pure, whatever is lovely, whatever is admirable—if anything is excellent or praiseworthy—think about such things." Ask students to consider how God would rate His approval of their favorite websites, TV shows and movies in light of this passage. Have them list their favorites from each category and then rank each from 1 to 10 based on how God would approve of them.

Website 1: _____

1	2	3	4	5	6	7	8	9	10
lowest									highest

Website 2: _____

1	2	3	4	5	6	7	8	9	10
lowest									highest

Website 3: _____

1	2	3	4	5	6	7	8	9	10
lowest									highest

TV show 1: _____

1	2	3	4	5	6	7	8	9	10
lowest									highest

TV show 2: _____

1	2	3	4	5	6	7	8	9	10
lowest									highest

TV show 3: _____

1	2	3	4	5	6	7	8	9	10
lowest									highest

Movie 1: _____

1	2	3	4	5	6	7	8	9	10
lowest									highest

Movie 2: _____

1	2	3	4	5	6	7	8	9	10
lowest									highest

Movie 3: _____

1	2	3	4	5	6	7	8	9	10
lowest									highest

Ask the group if there is anything that they feel they need to change about their viewing habits after doing this exercise.

message

You've probably heard the saying "The eyes are the windows to the soul." If our eyes can reveal our soul, can our souls be impacted by what we see?

Throughout this study, we've talked about honoring God with our bodies—with what goes into our bodies and what kinds of actions come out of them. You may think that the images that you consume are a lot less harmful to you than drugs, alcohol or sex could be—but you're wrong. Images have a powerful ability to drastically impact our self-image, our attitudes and outlooks and our standards of what we view as acceptable.

Some images we view are out of our control—an ad on the side of a bus, flyers that come in the mail, displays in a mall. But others—namely the websites that we visit, the magazines that we read and movies and TV shows we watch—are within our control.

So think about your image diet—those images you consume on a daily and weekly basis. Is your image diet pleasing to God? How can we keep our eyes and minds from impure images?

Read the following passage from Psalm 119:1-16,33-40. As you read, consider the following questions: (1) How can a person keep his or her way pure? (2) Is this writer's voice your voice too? (3) Do you deeply desire to obey God?

> *Blessed are they whose ways are blameless,*
> *who walk according to the law of the LORD.*
> *Blessed are they who keep his statutes*
> *and seek him with all their heart.*
> *They do nothing wrong;*
> *they walk in his ways.*
> *You have laid down precepts*
> *that are to be fully obeyed.*
> *Oh, that my ways were steadfast*
> *in obeying your decrees!*
> *Then I would not be put to shame*
> *when I consider all your commands.*
> *I will praise you with an upright heart*
> *as I learn your righteous laws.*
> *I will obey your decrees;*
> *do not utterly forsake me.*
>
> *How can a young man keep his way pure?*
> *By living according to your word.*

I seek you with all my heart;
do not let me stray from your commands.
I have hidden your word in my heart
that I might not sin against you.
Praise be to you, O LORD;
teach me your decrees.
With my lips I recount
all the laws that come from your mouth.
I rejoice in following your statutes
as one rejoices in great riches.
I meditate on your precepts
and consider your ways.
I delight in your decrees;
I will not neglect your word. . . .

Teach me, O LORD, to follow your decrees;
then I will keep them to the end.
Give me understanding, and I will keep your law
and obey it with all my heart.
Direct me in the path of your commands,
for there I find delight.
Turn my heart toward your statutes
and not toward selfish gain.
Turn my eyes away from worthless things;
preserve my life according to your word.
Fulfill your promise to your servant,
so that you may be feared.
Take away the disgrace I dread,
for your laws are good.
How I long for your precepts!
Preserve my life in your righteousness.

dig

1. How would you describe the psalm writer's attitude about
    following God's law?

    ....

    ....

    ....

    ....

    ....

2. Notice that for this psalmist, God's law is not some te-
    dious set of can'ts, don'ts and shouldn'ts designed to
    limit our freedoms. Instead, obedience to God's law pro-
    vides the framework for having a joyful, intimate and real
    relationship with Him. Read through these verses again
    and write down the specific actions that a person can take
    to keep himself or herself pure. Then list what you would
    need to do in order to accomplish each action. (Note that
    most of these actions will be between you and God.)

Actions to maintain purity	How to accomplish this
walk according to the law of the LORD	

3. The psalmist realizes that he cannot follow God success-
    fully on his own. What are some of the things the writer
    asks for from God?

    _____

    _____

    _____

    _____

    _____

    _____

4. In verse 37, the writer asks God to keep his "eyes away
    from worthless things." How do we determine what is
    worthwhile and what is worthless?

    _____

    _____

    _____

    _____

    _____

    _____

5. According to verse 40, what is the result when we follow
    God's law?

    _____

    _____

    _____

    _____

    _____

    _____

6. In Psalm 101, the writer also focuses on how he can be
    pure and blameless, looking at "no vile thing" (verse 3).
    Read the following passages from Psalm 101:1-7 in the
    left-hand column. Then, in the right-hand column, fill in
    the paraphrased version with applications that are spe-
    cific to your life.

Psalm 101	My Psalm 101
I will sing of your love and justice; to you, O LORD, I will sing praise.	God, I want to thank You for Your _____ and _____. I will give you praise.
I will be careful to lead a blameless life—when will you come to me? I will walk in my house with blameless heart.	I want to lead a blameless life—when will You come to me? Living in _____, I will walk with a blameless heart.
I will set before my eyes no vile thing. The deeds of faithless men I hate; they will not cling to me.	I won't look at _____ _____. I won't hang out with people who _____ _____.
Men of perverse heart shall be far from me; I will have nothing to do with evil.	I'll stay away from looking at things that _____ _____; I will have nothing to do with evil.
Whoever slanders his neighbor in secret, him will I put to silence; whoever has haughty eyes and a proud heart, him will I not endure.	I'll stand up to people who _____; I won't put up with people who _____ _____.

Psalm 101	My Psalm 101
My eyes will be on the faithful in the land, that they may dwell with me; he whose walk is blameless will minister to me.	Instead, my eyes will look at _____ _____. I'll look to _____ _____ as a role model and mentor to help hold me accountable as I strive to live.
No one who practices deceit will dwell in my house; no one who speaks falsely will stand in my presence.	Nothing that _____ will stay in my house; no images that are _____ will take up my time.

apply

1. In the chart below and on the following page, fill in the approximate number of hours each week that you do each leisure activity and each spiritual activity.

Leisure activity	Hours per week
Watching TV	
Non-school-related Internet surfing	
Online chatting	
Texting/on the phone	
Reading magazines	
TOTAL	

Spiritual activity	Hours per week
Reading the Bible	
Prayer	
Worship	
Service	
Youth group	
TOTAL	

2. Which table has the greatest number of hours? Based on this, where would you say your priorities lie?

    _____

    _____

    _____

    _____

    _____

3. Of course, watching TV shows, visiting websites and reading magazines are not necessarily bad in themselves. The question is in how much time you are doing these things versus how much time you are spending with God. Where you spend the most time will likely have the most impact on you, and it is impossible to grow closer to God, to seek His ways and to live according to His guidance if you are not spending time with Him. So, how can you create godly viewing habits? In the space below, develop some

guidelines for viewing the Internet, TV, movies, books and
magazines based on the Scripture passages you have read.

1. _____

2. _____

3. _____

4. _____

5. _____

reflect

1. What are the characteristics of a good movie or TV show?

_____
_____
_____
_____
_____
_____

2. What's your opinion of the movie rating system (G, PG,
PG-13, R, NC-17)? Is it fair? Is it too strict?

_____
_____
_____
_____
_____
_____
_____

3. What movies or TV programs have you seen recently that
    would be most Christ honoring? What recent movies or
    TV programs are the least Christ honoring?

    _____

    _____

    _____

    _____

    _____

    _____

    _____

4. Should your parents know about every movie that you
    see? Is it okay to see an R-rated movie without their
    knowledge?

    _____

    _____

    _____

    _____

    _____

    _____

5. Does God really care about which movies and TV shows
    you watch or websites you visit?

    _____

    _____

    _____

    _____

    _____

    _____

6. Is seeing violent, sexual, suggestive or crass images really a problem for people?

_____

_____

_____

_____

_____

7. Is there a difference between small kids, teenagers and adults seeing these kinds of images?

_____

_____

_____

_____

8. Besides the media we've talked about here (magazines, Internet, TV and movies), where else do you need to be on the lookout for unhealthy images?

_____

_____

_____

_____

_____

meditation

How can a young person stay pure?
By obeying your word.

PSALM 119:9, *NLT*

HOME WORD

HERE PARENTS GET REAL ANSWERS

Get Equipped with HomeWord...

LISTEN
HomeWord Radio
programs reach over 800 communities nationwide with *HomeWord with Jim Burns* – a daily ½ hour interview feature, *HomeWord Snapshots* – a daily 1 minute family drama, and *HomeWord this Week* – a ½ hour weekend edition of the daily program, and our one-hour program.

CLICK
HomeWord.com
provides advice and resources to millions of visitors each year. A truly interactive website, HomeWord.com provides access to parent newsletter, Q&As, online broadcasts, tip sheets, our online store and more.

READ
HomeWord Resources
parent newsletters, equip families and Churches worldwide with practical Q&As, online broadcasts, tip sheets, our online store and more. Many of these resources are also packaged digitally to meet the needs of today's busy parents.

ATTEND
HomeWord Events
Understanding Your Teenager, Building Healthy Morals & Values, Generation 2 Generation and Refreshing Your Marriage are held in over 100 communities nationwide each year. HomeWord events educate and encourage parents while providing answers to life's most pressing parenting and family questions.

A
Ministry *Jim Burns*
with

In response to the overwhelming needs of parents and families, Jim Burns founded HomeWord in 1985. HomeWord, a Christian organization, equips and encourages parents, families, and churches worldwide.

Find Out More
Sign up for our FREE daily
e-devotional and parent e-newsletter
at HomeWord.com, or call 800.397.9725.

HomeWord.com

Small Group Curriculum Kits

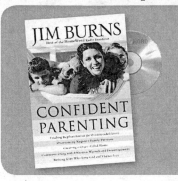

Confident Parenting Kit

This is a must-have resource for today's family! Let Jim Burns help you to tackle overcrowded lives, negative family patterns, while creating a grace-filled home and raising kids who love God and themselves.

Kit contains:
- 6 sessions on DVD featuring Dr. Jim Burns
- CD with reproducible small group leader's guide and participant guides
- poster, bulletin insert, and more

Creating an Intimate Marriage Kit

Dr. Jim Burns wants every couple to experience a marriage filled with A.W.E.: affection, warmth, and encouragement. He shows husbands and wives how to make their marriage a priority as they discover ways to repair the past, communicate and resolve conflict, refresh their marriage spiritually, and more!

Kit contains:
- 6 sessions on DVD featuring Dr. Jim Burns
- CD with reproducible small group leader's guide and participant guides
- poster, bulletin insert, and more

Parenting Teenagers for Positive Results

This popular resource is designed for small groups and Sunday schools. The DVD features real family situations played out in humorous family vignettes followed by words of wisdom by youth and family expert, Jim Burns, Ph.D.

Kit contains:
- 6 sessions on DVD featuring Dr. Jim Burns
- CD with reproducible small group leader's guide and participant guides
- poster, bulletin insert, and more

Teaching Your Children Healthy Sexuality Kit

Trusted family authority Dr. Jim Burns outlines a simple and practical guide for parents on how to develop in their children a healthy perspective regarding their bodies and sexuality. Promotes godly values about sex and relationships.

Kit contains:
- 6 sessions on DVD featuring Dr. Jim Burns
- CD with reproducible small group leader's guide and participant guides
- poster, bulletin insert, and more

Tons of helpful resources for youth workers, parents and youth. Visit our online store at www.HomeWord.com or call us at 800-397-9725

HOME WORD

WHERE PARENTS GET REAL ANSWERS

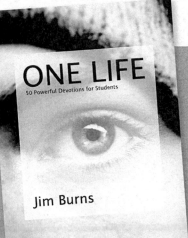

Small Group Curriculum Kits

Confirming Your Faith Kit

Rite-of-Passage curriculum empowers youth to make wise decisions...to choose Christ. Help them take ownership of their faith! Lead them to do this by experiencing a vital Christian lifestyle.

Kit contains:
- 13 engaging lessons
- Ideas for retreats and special Celebration
- Solid foundational Bible concepts
- 1 leaders guide and 6 student journals (booklets)

10 Building Blocks Kit

Learn to live, laugh, love, and play together as a family. When you learn the 10 essential principles for creating a happy, close-knit household, you'll discover a family that shines with love for God and one another! Use this curriculum to help equip families in your church.

Kit contains:
- 10 sessions on DVD featuring Dr. Jim Burns
- CD with reproducible small group leader's guide and participant guides
- poster and bulletin insert
- 10 Building Blocks book

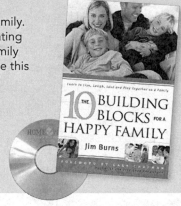

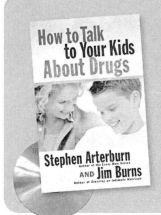

How to Talk to Your Kids About Drugs Kit

Dr. Jim Burns speaks to parents about the important topic of talking to their kids about drugs. You'll find everything you need to help parents learn and implement a plan for drug-proofing their kids.

Kit contains:
- 2 session DVD featuring family expert Dr. Jim Burns
- CD with reproducible small group leader's guide and participant guides
- poster, bulletin insert, and more
- How to Talk to Your Kids About Drugs book

Tons of helpful resources for youth workers, parents and youth. Visit our online store at www.HomeWord.com or call us at 800-397-9725

who is Jesus and why does He matter?

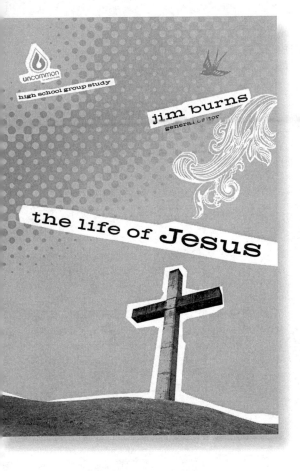

Everybody has heard of Jesus Christ, but a surprising number of teens have only a vague idea about who He really is and why He is so important. Don't you think it's time to fix that? Now you can, with the help of *The Life of Jesus,* part of the *Uncommon* youth study series created by veteran youth minister Jim Burns. Twelve sessions of youth-friendly Bible study will bring the life, teachings, death and resurrection of Jesus into focus and invite the teens in your group to take a long look at how He can made a difference in their lives.

the life of Jesus
Jim Burns, General Editor
ISBN 978.08307.47269

Available at Bookstores Everywhere!

Uncommon is a decidedly different program for Junior High and High School ministries. Now you can equip ministry leaders to hit the ground running with a complete package of proven and effective materials.

Gospel Light
God's Word for Your World™
www.gospellight.com